THEN
THE
AMERICANS
CAME

THEN
THE
AMERICANS
CAME

Voices from Vietnam

MARTHA HESS

FOUR WALLS EIGHT WINDOWS

NEW YORK/LONDON

Published by:

FOUR WALLS EIGHT WINDOWS

PO Box 548, Village Station

New York, N.Y. 10014

U.K. offices:

Four Walls Eight Windows/Turnaround

27 Horsell Road, London, N51 XL, England

First printing April 1993.

Library of Congress Cataloging-in-Publication Data:

Hess, Martha, 1948—

Then the Americans Came: Voices from Vietnam/Martha Hess.

p. cm

ISBN: 0-941423-92-1

1. Vietnamese Conflict, 1961-1975—Personal narratives. Vietnamese. I. Title

{DS559.5.H49 1993}

959.704'38--dc20   92-38999

                                CIP

Designed by Cindy LaBreacht.   Printed in the United States.

Photo page 2: Village guard tower, made of bamboo. Guards watch for U.S. bomber planes and warn the villagers to go to the shelters. Taken during the U.S. War. COURTESY VIETNAMESE PHOTOGRAPHERS ASSOCIATION (TRAN CU).

FOR
EMERICK

ACKNOWLEDGEMENTS

TO THE PEOPLE of Vietnam who opened their hearts, to the government officials who facilitated interviews and travel, to Nguyen Van Tuyen, my guide and friend, thank you for trusting me.

I am indebted to many people at home who provided information, advice and support. Special thanks to colleague and friend Tom Murray for years of valued feedback and constant encouragement. I thank the writer Gloria Emerson for countless hours of review and advice. Thank you, lawyer Franklin Siegel of the Center for Constitutional Rights, for legal advice. Merci, with love, Francis Foo. I am grateful for Cindy LaBreacht's fine, careful design. And I thank my lucky stars for publisher/editor John Oakes, without whose commitment and guidance there would be no book.

To my parents, who long ago taught me right from wrong and who have seen me through this project from beginning to end, you make the world a better place. Thank you.

PHOTO LEFT: **Child with a straw hat to protect him from bombing raids. Taken during the U.S. War.**
COURTESY VIETNAMESE PHOTOGRAPHERS ASSOCIATION (TRAN CU).

FOREWORD

AS I WRITE, there are some hopeful signs that the matter of the missing American M.I.A.'s will be put to rest. Think how hard it must have been for Vietnamese officials to appear solicitous about the fate of several hundred American servicemen when their own M.I.A.'s number 300,000! While we lost 58,000 of our people, they lost a million and a half of theirs.

When to these unhappy facts you add what for Americans are the two most unpleasant of all—that we had no business fighting the war in the first place, and, in the end, lost it—you can readily understand why it took so long for any American to produce a book of this kind. We've only begun to take in the rage and grief of our own troops, their sorrow reflected in the Vietnam Memorial, which manages so beautifully to honor the warriors without honoring the war.

Now isn't it time to hear from the other side? The cost of truth is never as high as the price of its denial. Martha Hess has written a painful book. Never mind; we are more alive in pain than in complacency. And of all swords, only the sword of truth can heal the wounds it inflicts.

William Sloane Coffin, Jr.

9

INTRODUCTION

"I can hear God saying to America,
you are too arrogant....
What strange liberators we are."

Martin Luther King, Jr.
April 30, 1967

I WENT TO VIETNAM for the first time in 1989, to touch
the land and people whose suffering had so influenced my
identity as an American, and to ask, what was the war like
for you?

The accounts and photographs that make up this
book were collected in 1990 and 1991. I have grouped
most people geographically. Veterans from the hospitals
are in a separate section. I have edited the accounts for
brevity, but the stories are as told, and names and places
have not been changed. Where full names are not
included, it is because people declined to provide them.
Because Vietnamese names will not be familiar to most
readers, I have indicated sex by "Mr." or "Mrs."

PHOTOS PAGES 8 AND LEFT:
**Amerasians at the Amerasian Transit Center in Ho Chi Minh City,
waiting to go to the United States. 1991.** PHOTO BY M. HESS.

I worked with a guide from the national tourist office, Nguyen Van Tuyen. We drove from Ho Chi Minh City up the coast to Quang Ngai province, where a lot of fighting took place. We stopped at what is left of My Lai, which is to say, nothing. Some monuments and a little museum have been built, and a hospital was donated by a charity in Washington—there are no funds to run it. We drove on to Danang and Hue and then Quang Tri province, where the biggest battles in the American war were fought, crossed the Ben Hai River at the 17th parallel, and passed through Vinh Linh. Vinh Linh was attacked by sea, by land, and by air. We stopped in the province of Thanh Hoa, and ended up in Hanoi. We also drove west across the mountains to Dien Bien Phu, where the French were defeated in the battle of 1954. I didn't expect to learn much there about the American War in Vietnam, but I was wrong. The city had been razed by bombs dropped from U.S. planes flying back to Thailand from missions over Hanoi and Haiphong, and French war matériel lying scattered about since 1954 is stamped "Made in U.S.A."

Often we would just stop on the road and approach people who appeared to be of an age to remember the war. One person led to another, and onlookers joined the conversation. In Thanh Hoa, for example, I never got further than the visitors' compound. We had come late for lunch, and the cook, the medic, various staff—all women—were talking with one another at a large table. They were curious about me, naturally, and after some banter in their language, Tuyen, my guide, persuaded one woman to talk into my tape recorder, and three others followed. It was a quiet afternoon and they hadn't expected to spend it looking back to those dark times, but they made room at their table and they spoke softly, and then thanked me for listening.

Other times we had to obtain permits to go to villages, or we had the assistance of the People's Committee of a town or a Commission on War Crimes or a provincial museum, and I was provided with photographs and statistics and taken to meet war victims. I had no affiliations or credentials, and I traveled on a tourist visa.

It is only with Tuyen's collaboration, and, through him, with that of the Vietnamese people, that I was able to make this record. People opened their hearts and their deepest sorrows to a stranger, come, after all, from the land of the enemy. They showed me their wounds and they showed me their anger and their hatred and their amazing capacity to forgive. They wept, and they brought out old snapshots of lost loved ones. They introduced me to their children and invited me to their tables, and they took my hands in theirs. They asked me to tell the people in America what our bombs and our napalm and our guns had done, and to tell them we should come back in friendship. Natives of the North talked about the bombing. People with no legs, no arms, a few fingers missing, told me what happened. Others recounted months and years of torture, beatings, and imprisonment. Soldiers described their suffering and their love of freedom. Families recalled missing sons. Villagers spoke of massacres they had survived. Mothers told me how they lost their children. I heard how Americans raped young women and grandmothers and little girls, how they tortured and killed, how they destroyed entire villages and sometimes took the wounded to hospitals in their helicopters.

In the beginning Tuyen said, "If you've never seen war, you will never know how terrible it is, same thing if you never saw snow, you can't know how white it is." I learned how right he is, and understand less than ever why wars exist. This book is about our war crimes, and about the crime of war. In the United States, while public attention has focused on the American soldier as a victim of "misguided" policy, there seems to be little concern or even curiosity about the people of that faraway land who were the object of our country's apocalyptic wrath. Those victims are dismissed with a flick of the wrist. An American vet who frequently travels to Vietnam told me that "for the Vietnamese vets the war is over, they forgot all about it." Kids today are surprised to learn that we lost that war.

Did Rambo rewrite history? Because of racism and humiliation, Vietnam remains a faceless nation to Americans and the extent of its people's suffering at our hands is unknown. We must acknowledge our shame and accept responsibility for the actions of our government, so that the next time we can stand up and say no. We demand no less from the Germans. We have sought absolution from our war against the Vietnamese in other wars, on other faceless people. Real absolution can only be world peace.

One beautiful day my guide and I went to visit pagodas outside Hanoi. We passed through very small villages with nothing to them but a lot of foul-smelling water, and wet mud underfoot, and thatched houses with dried-mud walls. There were all manner of hard-working people, breaking their backs for a lifetime, as their ancestors had done for four thousand years, fighting that muddy earth for survival. They looked up to see what the children were shrieking about—it was me, bumping through their ancient land in a beat-up old Russian car, the blue-eyed devil.

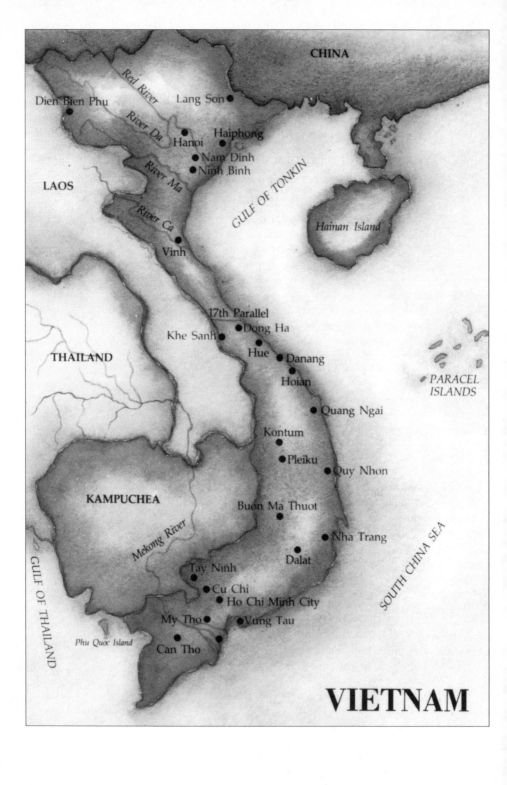

A BIT OF HISTORY

WHAT IS KNOWN IN VIETNAM as the American War was the bloody culmination of two thousand years of resistance to foreign invaders. The Chinese came first, and the Vietnamese fought them for ten centuries.

The French came in the 19th century and conquered the kingdoms of Indochina. Putting down sporadic resistance, they governed until 1940, when Germany defeated France and the Vichy authorities in Indochina let the Japanese military move in without firing a shot. President Franklin D. Roosevelt protested the Japanese aggression and sought economic sanctions. This early friction eventually led to the attack on Pearl Harbor. During the war, a nationalist coalition called the Viet Minh (an abbreviation for the League for Vietnamese Independence), led by the communist Ho Chi Minh, began an underground resistance that left them in effective control of the country when Japan surrendered in 1945. They later came to be known in the United States and South Vietnam as the Viet Cong, or V.C.

Ho Chi Minh began treaty negotiations with the new DeGaulle regime in Paris, but in November 1946 the French bombarded the northern port city of Haiphong, and the war was on. The Truman Administration, on the

17

pretext of fighting communism, helped finance and supply the French War, which ended in 1954 with a French defeat in the great battle at Dien Bien Phu.

The Geneva Agreements that year provided for the departure of the French and the temporary partition of Vietnam at the 17th parallel, with the Viet Minh administering the North, and forces that had served the French administering the South. They also provided for national elections to be held by 1956 at the latest, and the country would then be reunified. But, as President Eisenhower noted in his memoirs, the Viet Minh would have won, so the elections were never held. The U.S.-sponsored regime of Ngo Dinh Diem sought permanency by repressing the opposition—through massive killings, detentions, and torture—which led to public demonstrations and the rise of a new guerrilla movement. At the time of partition, most of the Catholics of Vietnam had gone to the South. Under Diem, Buddhism was repressed. There were mass protests, including the self-immolation by fire of several Buddhist monks on city streets in South Vietnam. Until the end of the war, Buddhists were active in the movement for peace and an end to foreign domination.

The bad news from Saigon prompted President John F. Kennedy to approve the overthrow of Diem, who died in the coup on November 1, 1963, just three weeks before J.F.K. was himself assassinated. During the Kennedy Administration, the number of American military "advisers" had risen to 10,000, and the CIA conducted a secret war in Laos in an effort to cut the Ho Chi Minh Trail, a network of paths and roads through the jungle and mountains down which supplies and then troops came from the North. The military dictators who took over in Saigon were no more effective than Diem. Then, in August 1964, President Lyndon B. Johnson announced that the North Vietnamese had attacked two destroyers in the Gulf of Tonkin—many historians say it never happened—and obtained Congressional approval of a resolution, which had been drafted before the Tonkin Incident, authorizing him to retaliate.

That was the beginning of what Americans call the Vietnam War. It became a holocaust. From the first ground units of combat troops, U.S. forces grew to over half a million men. More bombs were dropped on Vietnam than fell in Europe during World War II. Millions of gallons of defoliants and napalm ravaged the forests and rice fields, the villages and their inhabitants. Villages were razed, people killed, raped, tortured, jailed, relocated into concentration camps. The massacre at My Lai on March 16, 1968, was one of many.

Repeatedly, the Pentagon announced that victory was near, that "there was light at the end of the tunnel," but kept asking for more men. The Tet Offensive, a general uprising in the South which began on the Vietnamese New Year in January 1968, was put down, but it destroyed many illusions. Along with worldwide and domestic opposition to the war, it caused L.B.J. to halt the troop buildup, call for peace talks, and withdraw from the presidential campaign. The war continued nonetheless. President Richard M. Nixon slowly reduced the number of U.S. ground forces, but stepped up the bombing of the North and South, raided Laos and Cambodia and, still fighting communism, continued the war for over four more years. Another justification by this time was the emotional issue of American prisoners of war and M.I.A.'s, which is used to this day to isolate Vietnam diplomatically and economically.

A month after the massive bombings of northern cities in December 1972, what the Vietnamese call "Dien Bien Phu in the air," Nixon signed a peace agreement along lines that had been proposed years earlier. That agreement included a promise, never fulfilled, of $3.25 billion in U.S. reconstruction aid. With most U.S. forces gone, the South Vietnamese regime survived only until April 30, 1975, when Saigon was liberated and the last Americans left.

Vietnam was united and at peace, for the most part. In late 1978, the Vietnamese responded to mass killings by the Khmer Rouge in villages close to the Cambodian border by invading Cambodia and defeating Pol Pot's regime. In 1979, an incursion by the Chinese at Vietnam's northern border resulted in a two-month war.

The American War in Vietnam, Laos and Cambodia caused the deaths of 58,000 Americans and unknown millions of Indochinese.

NORTH

OF THE

17TH

PARALLEL

Nguyen Thanh Mai. 1990. PHOTO BY M. HESS.
OVERLEAF: Soldiers marching south along the Ho Chi Minh Trail.
Taken during the U.S. War. COURTESY VIETNAMESE PHOTOGRAPHERS
ASSOCIATION (TRAN CU).

Vinh Linh

MRS. NGUYEN THANH MAI

THE WAR STARTED in the North in 1964, the fifth of August. At that time, I was nine years old, and lived in Dong Hoi. We knew when we were going to be bombed, and the children and older people were taken out the day before. My mother, a nurse, and my father, who was in the army, stayed in the city with my two older sisters. I went to a village about twenty kilometers north, to a friend of my father. They bombed for only one hour that afternoon, but the whole city was destroyed. It was a very small city, very nice. In one hour it was completely destroyed.

We were lucky. My mother suffered from a concussion. She bled through the mouth. At the time, she was four months pregnant, and she lost the child. Everything was gone, our house, our possessions, everything. I remember, about ten weeks later I had a chance to return and I saw it once more—nothing.

We went to live near a forest, my family and all the other survivors, and we stayed there from 1964 until the liberation of the South. We were bombed nearly every day. You know, it was a very important place, about sixty,

25

seventy kilometers north of the 17th parallel. The Northern soldiers passed through on their way to the front, and wounded people were being carried back.

We cut wood and built a house, but most of the time we stayed in a tunnel. The house was a facade, just somewhere to come out to sometimes. You may not believe how we were bombed nearly every day, sometimes three, four times a day. I had one friend—ten people in her family, eight died. Only two sisters are still alive.I stayed in that village by the forest for seven, eight years, and the bombing was continual.

Then our school was moved further north. Just the pupils were moved, no family, no parents, no sisters. One day a village about three kilometers away was bombed, and many, many people died. We were strong, young, and we went to help. We saw a family that had been having dinner, and they died around a table of food and rice. There was a baby still feeding at her mother's bosom, but the mother was dead. Another woman took the baby home to raise like a daughter. At that time we knew war, only war, and we loved each other very deeply. We were ready to help each other. We didn't mind hardships, we wanted only to help each other. There were many sad cases like this, so sad.

We rationed everything, medicine, food, fuel. We lacked nearly everything. We used medicine from the forest. We learned first from our grandfathers, the older generation, and then we learned from the war. We became wise, also clever. We found wild plants in the forest. Sometimes they weren't healthy to eat, but we were hungry. We might share a chicken or a pig. Sometimes a buffalo used for plowing would be wounded by bombs, and we would take it home, and kill it, and share the meat. Money was nothing. We didn't use money for a long time. What could we buy? So if a cow died, all the people in the village would eat it together. If we had something, we shared it with each other or else gave it to the soldiers. If we found a wounded soldier, and often we didn't know who this soldier was, we would take him home. We didn't have enough food to eat, but we took a little bit of rice to make a soup for the wounded soldier. The children would sit and look at the soldier eating, not angry, only hungry.

We got two kilograms of rice a month for five people. We had manioc and grew sweet potatoes, and we had pineapples and other fruits, though sometimes our food was destroyed by the bombs.

There were many different kinds of bombs—100 kilograms, 1,000 kilograms. Fragmentation bombs came right over as we hid in the tunnels. There were so many planes, and sometimes I could see their eyes, that is, the eyes of the American pilots.

Today, my parents are very weak. The bombing destroyed their health. My mother was hit directly three, four times. She lost consciousness, and often bled.

Sometimes we stayed in the house, but the house was already half underground, and the tunnel was deep. When we heard the planes we went down into the tunnels. Often people didn't get to the tunnels in time, and they died. School was held in the tunnels, babies were born there. How could we live inside a tunnel for such a long time, nine, eight years?

All the villagers helped families bury their dead. So many died. We covered them, simply. We didn't even have coffins. How could we get coffins for the dead?

Rice was rationed at a place ten, fifteen kilometers from where we lived, and each family would send someone for it. In my family there was no son, and usually my sisters went. One time my brother-in-law—though he wasn't my brother-in-law yet—said he would get the rice. Those people were bombed. Many people were killed and my brother-in-law was wounded. We tried to heal his wounds, but he still has fragments in his body.

Dong Hoi is near the sea. One river, the Nhat Le River, runs alongside the city, very nice. Dong Hoi is a small town and it was bombed, but people returned. There was a village between the river and the sea, and to get to it we needed a boat. Most of the village people were fishermen and they had boats, but when the pilots saw people on the boats, of course they bombed. So only a few dared to row the boats. One of those people was a woman named Me Suot. We loved her deeply, and that is why we called her Me, meaning mother. She carried people, food, weapons, everything, until she was killed by bombs. Me Suot is a national heroine.

During the war we read little books that told of the good deeds people do. A series of these books was called *One Hundred Good Things*. The stories set examples, like the wife who stayed in the fields and worked, and also helped her husband at the front—sent medicine, suffered, and waited for her husband. Some women waited twenty years. When I was young, I wanted to be like that. I

THEN THE AMERICANS CAME

wanted to love a soldier who would go off to fight and then I would wait at home. Some of my friends were soldiers. Fourteen, sixteen years old they were already soldiers. We liked them but they never fell in love with us, because they were soldiers. They had nothing, and they didn't know where or when they would die. Or they kept their love locked in their hearts. When they went to the South they might die, and their sweethearts would wait for nothing. Would you believe, after soldiers came back from the South—no legs, no arms, and some girls I knew fell in love. They were very young, sixteen, twenty, sad, maybe even wanted to die. And a girl would come and say something soft, and they would fall in love, and sometimes they married. I saw that myself.

I also had girlfriends who went to work in the forest to build the Ho Chi Minh Trail. They were young and beautiful and smart. They stayed in the forest for ten, fifteen years, and when the country was liberated and they came back, they were over thirty. In our country they were already old. They had no skills, because they had had no time for learning, and nobody to fall in love with them. They had lost their youth. Truly, these girls had given their lives for their country. For the boys that's no problem, but for the girls there is nothing.

We did everything we could to liberate the South. For example, if a bridge was destroyed, the families who lived near that bridge would take everything from their house—beams and everything, to patch the bridge, for the army to pass. And if it rained, families would then have no house, no shelter. We were all ready to give, and I think that is how we won the war.

I don't know why we were so strong. When the soldiers needed help, we carried rice, weapons. When we had a shipload from China, we claimed it quickly in case there was a bombing raid. Some of my friends would put a hundred kilograms on their backs and run—many, many times. When the soldiers needed wood for the roads, we carried it. We were ready. We didn't know about being tired. We dug so many tunnels, a long tunnel to the school, one house to house, so that when we were bombed the survivors could run still through the tunnels for help.

I saw American pilots captured. Sometimes people would come to beat them, people who had lost loved ones and were angry. But the army wouldn't allow this. They were told, this pilot will be punished by the authorities, not by you.

Once I saw a young girl, a guerrilla, leading an American pilot. She was very small. We are small people, you see. The American pilot was very tall. She looked proud as they walked. The man kept his head down, only looked at the ground, but the girl looked very proud. We have poems about that.

Now, when I think of the past, I am amazed. Sometimes I think, how could we suffer, how could we finally achieve victory? Sometimes I can't believe we made it, because the Americans were very strong. They had all kinds of weapons, and food. They had enough. But the Vietnamese soldiers sometimes would have no food for a week, sometimes only a few vegetables and fruit, wild fruit.

Although, there was always manioc. It's easy to grow in Vietnam. We planted it all over the forest for the soldiers to cook and eat the root. Before they left, for each one they took, the soldiers planted another, for the next ones that passed through. That's how we won the war. We were clever.

On the Ho Chi Minh Trail and in the forest we had three sayings: *di khong dau,* to walk without footprints; *nau khong khoi,* to cook without smoke; and *noi khong tieng,* to speak without sound—you know why? There were these special trees, plastic trees that could hear every sound, and if they heard people, they would bomb them.

Sometimes my own family will talk about the war. We say, how can it be that we are still alive, because they bombed and bombed and bombed, that nobody in our family died? One woman had seven sons, and when the first one grew up she sent him off to war, and he died. She cried and cried. And then she sent the next one, and the third and the fourth, and they each died. Six boys died, and then she let the last one go, because his brothers had gone before him, for his brothers. I know the love between a mother and son, and even now sometimes I cry when I think about it. I ask myself, if I lost my son, how could I live? But she gave the first and the second, then three, four, five, six, and finally the seventh, the last one.

Working the fields, close to guns and bomb shelters. Taken during the U.S. War. COURTESY VIETNAMESE PHOTOGRAPHERS ASSOCIATION (TRAN CU).

MRS. NGUYEN THI THIET

THE BOMBING started in Vinh Linh on February 8, 1965. In the beginning the Americans bombed the hospitals, the schools, and the military camp. At first, not many people were killed. The worst was after 1965. So many were killed, especially in 1972.

People from Quang Tri Province had been evacuated north to Vinh Linh because they thought it was safer than the South. They were wrong. Some days, twelve, thirteen, fourteen people were killed. In an area of a kilometer or two, in a single morning the Americans would drop sixty, seventy bombs.

Mostly, people lived underground. The people of Vinh Linh are farmers, and still went to the fields to work every day. But when the planes came they escaped to the tunnels right by the fields. The women and young people always carried guns with them, to shoot at planes.

I was ten years old at the time of the second bombing, in 1972. School was always held in the shelter. The children couldn't come up. I lived seven days a week underground.

Toxic chemicals and defoliants were dropped, and a lot of napalm. Many people today still have scars from napalm bombs. There were different kinds of fragmentation bombs, some the size of a fist. Even now people get killed from small, unexploded bombs. Wounded people were looked after by their families, or by the community if they had no children or relatives. The dead were buried everywhere, without coffins. Three people died in my family.

The Americans cannot repay this debt, because it's too big.

MR. NGUYEN THE CHAT

THEY BOMBED so much here because it is the border between North and South. The Americans wanted to stop the transportation of weapons and supplies. The worst time was 1967, 1968, especially in 1968 during *Mau Than,* the Tet Offensive, when the Americans stepped up the war. They bombed schools and hospitals, places crowded with people. In Vinh Quang village, one hundred and two people were killed by one bomb. We dug up the shelter and found sixty-four bodies, and we made a common grave.

There were fourteen people in my family, and now there are only four. My mother was killed when I was thirteen. We buried her with the help of neighbors. We just buried the dead, no coffin or anything. The bombing was too fierce. Before the war Vinh Quang was so beautiful, but all that remains is a wasteland.

Many planes were shot down. The people lived underground, and they came to work with guns on their backs.

In a restaurant in the city of Dong Hoi, we approached these people at their table, and they offered their recollections of the bombing.

MR. NGUYEN VAN HOA

DONG HOI WAS EVACUATED but some of us stayed. My family was the last to leave. Then they bombed the evacuation center, and some of my relatives were killed. When we went to live in the countryside, I continued to attend school. Our classroom was connected to a tunnel, and when the planes came we would go down. The farmers, when the planes came they would go down, and when they were gone they returned to the fields. Of course we were always hungry, and we ate our meals quickly. Life was harsh. When it rained the shelters got wet and dirty. One by one, step by step, we drained the tunnels. When people were killed, some had coffins, some didn't. Many, many times, if the bombs hit the shelter directly, we couldn't find the victims, not even pieces. Whenever a plane was shot down, the local militia arrived to capture the pilot and to hold the people back, because they were afraid the American would be killed.

Dong Hoi has just been rebuilt in the last two years. During the war it was flattened. Only the water tower and the church bell tower were left.

The old church bell tower in Dong Hoi. 1990. PHOTO BY M. HESS.

MR. TRUONG THU

MY PARENTS were killed in 1967, and it took us two days to find their bodies. I was twelve years old at the time, and I went to live with my older sister. During evacuation, the government gave me eight *dong* every month—that's like 8,000 today [*about one U.S. dollar*]. I was evacuated three times, once from Thanh Hoa, where the orphanage was, and twice from here.

MRS. LUU

I SAW A PLANE shot down. And when the pilot was caught, the villagers came to kill him, and were kept back by the local forces. There was a family in my village, six people were killed, four children and their parents were killed by one bomb.

The Americans had every kind of bomb. The phosphorus bomb made my brother very ugly. He has a wife and children now. He and his wife loved each other before he was burned by the phosphorus bomb, but now he looks terrible. He went to Hanoi to have his face fixed, but it is still not too good. If you stay in Quang Binh province, you will see many scars.

I was lucky. Who can escape from bombs? Every day there was bombing, every day you listened for the sound of the bombs, every day you might not escape, and every day you know you might die at any time.

This is my daughter. After 1975, her father came back from the front, and we gave birth to this baby. We waited until peacetime.

Nghe Tinh Province

MR. CAU NGOC XUAN

In the village of Dien Chau, on the road from Vinh to Thanh Hoa, we visited the caretaker of the Cuong Temple—Peacock Temple.

OUR TEMPLE WAS never bombed. It is very sacred. It is protected by the spirit of the king. All around here was bombed into zero. There was nothing left. Our houses would burn and collapse, so we had to sleep out in the fields. The planes flew over us often, and if the Americans thought there was a hospital, a military company, battalion, or a base, they would bomb. If we gathered in the fields to work, we were also bombed. Many people here were killed, so we worked at night.

Day and night we lived in the tunnels. They had fragmentation bombs—we called them mother bombs. There was a bomb we called the slow bomb. It is dropped, then only after some days it explodes, or if you touch it. And they used napalm.

I remember the first time the Americans came to bomb us, 1968, the seventh July moon. That is a day of mercy for the dead. We were in the middle of our ancestral festival celebrations. The Americans bombed our village on that day, the day when we pray for the souls of the dead, especially for those who have no graves. Six people were killed in one family, and they couldn't even find the pieces.

It was difficult to farm. We couldn't produce rice, and everything was being stored for the front. We ate vegetable porridge or manioc. In the daytime we couldn't cook because the smoke could be seen, and at night we couldn't cook because the fire could be seen. When they saw smoke or fire and knew there were people, they would drop the bombs. They bombed the buffalos and cows, too, the most valuable possession of the Vietnamese family. My family lost two buffalos. And they destroyed our water conservation system, the *Son Duong* project.

Now there are a lot of disabled people who must live off their children and families. The government can help only a little.

All the young people joined the war. Everyone volunteered to go to the front but they took only the young ones, not older people like me. But we helped the soldiers, took food and supplies to the soldiers, and helped to make shelters and strongholds for the cannons to shoot the planes. Everyone helped. The people in this village shot down two planes. When the pilots were captured the people came, and if the army had let them, they would have been killed in seconds. But our soldiers kept them away.

After a bombing we would have a mass organization of the older people, of the farmers, of the young people, and of the women. We have these associations, and we helped each other. For instance, the Women's Union would take shifts to cook, to help people, look after the children, to help bombing victims.

Tuyen says, "There is a Vietnamese proverb: Use good leaves to cover the torn ones."

I don't hate Americans. I hate the policy of invading other countries. And the debt, the distribution from the Paris Agreements, why haven't they given us anything? We are very poor because of the war. The Americans don't see how they destroyed everything, and they won't pay their debt. I listen to the radio and hear how the Americans still have an embargo on our economy, and have no diplomatic relations with us. That's not right.

This is the Vietnamese people's land. Why did the Americans come to destroy us and make war, and why don't they help now to rebuild our country? I am a farmer, I stay here. And I ask a simple question. Why did the Americans come here to destroy homes and kill people? And I ask you, who invaded who? If Vietnam decided to invade America they would have to send troops—the distance is far, thousands of kilometers. I ask you, if I came to your land to destroy and burn your houses, how would you feel? So I say, when the Americans came here to fight and destroy the Vietnamese people, they were wrong. The Vietnamese were not wrong to defend their land. And when the Americans lost the war, why didn't they want to have relations with us?

The American people didn't make the mistake, it was the government. American people and Vietnamese people are alike, we work in the fields, we till the land. We have blood, we have hair, we have skin. Since we are all the same, we should be friends. Johnson and Nixon should ask pardon of the Vietnamese people and help to restore our country, as the Paris Agreements say.

I live in this temple now, close to the spirits, so I don't know anything.

Carrying bombing victims out from shelters in Vinh Linh. 1967.

Hoang Thi Ai. 1990. PHOTO BY M. HESS.

Thanh Hoa

MRS. HOANG THI AI

IN THE FIRST WAR, mostly they bombed bridges, ferries, roads, military bases. But in the second war the Americans bombed civilians. They started in 1965. I must have been about twenty-one. I was going to medical school fifteen kilometers from here, and I saw them bomb the Van Ferry, which took civilians from one side of the river to the other. Then they dropped a lot of bombs near my school and we were evacuated. I became an assistant doctor in 1966, and later joined the local artillery forces. Three times I helped capture U.S. pilots. When they parachuted down, many airplanes would still be flying overhead, so we tied them to a tree and waited for the planes to go away. Then we brought them to Thanh Hoa and from there they were taken to Hanoi. Maybe those pilots are back in America now.

I worked in a clinic. We had practically no medicine, just some penicillin and streptomycin. For napalm victims we had only a burn spray. We sprayed their bodies and took them to the hospital. But here they dropped a lot of fragmentation bombs, to kill the people. We could only bandage them and bring them to the hospital. We carried the wounded on a bamboo stretcher, on foot through the fields, thirty kilometers. You couldn't use the road because of the airplanes.

We were very hungry. There was nothing to eat, no rice. Most people lived on manioc and sweet potato. But we fought very well. They say, Vietnamese people have no food but they can fight.

I knew a woman who had only one son to work the land, and a bomb dropped and killed him. She went mad.

Mrs. Dung lived near me. She had five children that were evacuated to the hills here, the Dragon Mountains. All five children were killed by bombs, and she was left alone. She became weak and sick, and some years ago she died of cancer.

Women helped each other. When someone was wounded we would bring food, cook for them, help with the housework. The Women's Union in Vietnam is very important. Every village, every hamlet, every office has one.

In 1971, I had my second daughter, and we were evacuated. When I was called back to the clinic, I remember riding a bicycle with my six-month-old baby seventy kilometers. I was always afraid. One time I was sure I would die, the planes flew overhead and bombed right next to me. Through the burning, the destruction, the smoke—I could see nothing.

MRS. NGUYEN THI CUE

I AM VERY HAPPY that you have come here to build a bridge of friendship between America and Vietnam.

One of my brothers was sacrificed in the war. My village is near the Ham Rong Bridge, and there the bombing was very fierce. I was thirteen years old in 1965. One afternoon a group of planes came to bomb the Ham Rong Bridge, but didn't make a direct hit, and all the bombs dropped on my village. In one family a mother and her four children were killed. Only their father—he had no legs because he was wounded during the French time—was away from the house. My cousin went away to be a teacher. The day of his return the village was bombed and his head was blown off. We found only his body. He was buried with no head.

Tuyen says, "In Vietnam, we call that a ghost without a head. The children are very afraid of that ghost."

I had an uncle, he was in the civilian militia. They were bombing ships on the river near my house, and he ran to his fishing boat for his rifle. He got hit and his leg was cut off. The leg floated up by the boat. He was carried fifteen kilometers to the hospital. He died later.

MRS. PHUNG THI TAI

EVEN NOW I CRY when I remember the war.

My husband was killed in 1968, and my younger brother too, both at the battle of Khe Sanh. We heard the news at the same time. I was at the evacuation center. I went back to the village, and they had a ceremony to remember all those who died at the front. So we formed a body out of leaves, with a coconut shell for the head. A simple funeral.

I was very lonely after that. Later I remarried and had one child. I am already a grandmother. But the love that was once alive, we can never forget.

One time, at Sam Son Beach, near here, they were shelling from a ship, and I saw two people with their heads cut off. Another time, they bombed our evacuation center, forty kilometers from here, at Ngum Hill. It was fierce. There was one woman, I remember, who gave birth in the field, with leeches biting her. It was difficult to get back and forth from the center because the Americans were always bombing the road, and the cars and buses had to travel without lights.

I wanted to tell you something that I saw myself and of my own loss, but the war was not just about me. It was the whole country. We all lived with great difficulties and suffering. The poverty and hard conditions that still exist today are because of the war.

You are an American woman. You want to know about the war in Vietnam and bring the crimes of the U.S. before the American public, and I thank you for that. Not only Vietnamese people or Vietnamese women, but all people in the world hate war. So who starts wars?

Mr. Kung. 1990. PHOTO BY M. HESS.

Around Hanoi

MR. KUNG

EVERY VILLAGE HAD A GONG, usually made from a bomb. When they beat the gong we went down to the shelters. During the Nixon War, they beat the gong all the time. Sometimes I wouldn't go to the shelter, but stayed behind, in bed. Odd thing, sometimes we didn't care.

Pham Dinh Bang. 1990. PHOTO BY M. HESS.

We talked to two men just outside the beautiful
Thay Phuong Pagoda in Thach That Hanoi village,
about sixty kilometers from Hanoi.

MR. PHAM DINH BANG

I JOINED THE ARMY in 1969. After six months I went to
Cambodia and fought the Americans there. I remember
when the Americans brought troops and first bombed
Cambodia. Many people were killed. They bombed civilians, just like in Vietnam. Wherever they saw people, they
bombed. I stayed there until 1975. I lost a lot of friends
from bombings and contamination by toxic chemicals,
and was myself injured and exposed. But I always believed
that we would win.

The army informed my family that I had died, that I
was sacrificed at the front. But I came back.

MR. DICH

I WANT TO KNOW if the American veterans were affected by defoliants and toxic chemicals, because during all the years we marched south, the American army used them to clear the forests. The soldiers who fought at the front, south of Quang Tri, suffered sperm damage. If you go to Dac Lac and Pleiku, the people there can show you exactly where the Americans dropped the stuff. You can still find containers full of toxic chemicals. These "bitter mines," as we called them, since they leave a bitter taste, were very dangerous. After the war, my second child was born and died right away. My wife was strong, but the child was deformed. With the third child, the same thing, but the Swedish Hospital in Hanoi saved him. He is only four years old but he has intestinal problems. Doctors think his intestines are shrinking. They say when he grows up they can fix it. Now they give him medication.

The worst time was the bombing in 1972. It destroyed Kham Tien Street in Hanoi, and Bach Mai Hospital. But a lot of people were killed in the South, too, in battle. We would draw a map to remember where we buried our comrades.

The Americans came to Vietnam to conduct a war, and to kill Vietnamese people. That means they were the aggressors. The puppet soldiers were also Vietnamese but they were Americanized, meaning they listened to the Americans and took up arms against their own people. For those soldiers we have more sympathy than hatred. To this day we think of the Americans as the enemy. Our children have no fathers. The Americans killed a generation. They owe us, for the next generation.

MR. NGUYEN QUOC HUNG

I WAS EIGHT or nine years old in 1964, at the time of the
Tonkin Bay crisis, and we were evacuated south to my
parents' native land in Nghe Tinh. But the bombing was
so fierce we went to the shelter twenty times a day. I went
to school in the evening. When they beat the gong, we all
went to the shelter. We had oil lamps, no electricity. I
remember, when we went to school we had straw hats to
protect us from pieces of shell and bombs that came
down. In the city we had worn bright clothing, but when
we got to the countryside we didn't want to be seen by the
planes. It was a dangerous time. I was evacuated four
times in the first war.

In 1972, I went to Kham Thien Street in Hanoi, to
help collect pieces of bodies that had been scattered
about. Then I joined the army. We traveled day after day
into the South, with twenty-five-kilogram packs on our
backs and blisters on our feet. Along the Ho Chi Minh
Trail we grew manioc. We would dig it up and have a
good meal, and plant another before we left. We ate the
manioc that our comrades in the past had planted, and six
months later others would come and eat the manioc we
had planted. The first time I met a South Vietnamese soldier I was surprised to see he was about forty years old,
but his identity card said he was thirteen. He had been
forced to join the army three times, and the third time he
had tried to get out of it by saying he was too young. He
had no spirit left to fight. In North Vietnam you would
never find that.

Schoolchildren going to the shelter as the gong announces a bombing raid. Taken during the U.S. War. COURTESY VIETNAMESE PHOTOGRAPHERS ASSOCIATION (TRAN CU).

MR. NGUYEN DUC HANH

Mr. Hanh heads the War Crimes Investigation Commission of Hanoi.

THE UNITED STATES "war of destruction" over Vietnam started in 1964, but the Americans officially began bombing Hanoi on April 17, 1965. The last day of bombing was on December 29, 1972. There were two hundred days of bombing in total. In 1966 they bombed Hanoi for twenty-two days; in 1967, ninety-two days; in the beginning of 1968, thirty-five days. That was the Johnson period. In the Nixon period, they bombed from April 16, 1972 until December 29, 1972. During the twelve days of bombing at Christmas that year alone, 2,027 people were killed, 263 missing, 1,355 wounded.

Of the 102 villages in the suburbs of Hanoi, all were bombed. One hundred and sixteen schools and thirty kindergartens and nursery schools were bombed. One hundred and fifteen pagodas, churches and temples were bombed. One hundred and ten factories and businesses were bombed. One hundred and fifty warehouses were bombed. One hundred and six streets and sixty neighborhoods were bombed. Fifty-three hospitals and clinics were bombed. The dikes were bombed in seventy-one places—they are very important for flood control. All systems of transportation, communication, railway stations, bridges, and airports were bombed. Fifteen embassies were bombed.

An Duong is a working class neighborhood in the north of Hanoi. It is densely populated. In the morning of December 21, 1972, more than six hundred bombs were dropped. The neighborhood, including homes, schools, hospital, shops, was destroyed. One hundred and seventy-one people were killed, 151 wounded.

Kham Thien Street, which dates back to the tenth century, is one of the most crowded neighborhoods in Hanoi. Thirty thousand people live here. Three thousand bombs were dropped on Kham Thien on the evening of December 26, 1972. Two hundred eighty-seven people were killed, and 290 were wounded.

Bach Mai Hospital was built by the French. After 1954, it was restored and became the biggest hospital in North Vietnam. It was bombed four times.

Five hundred and fifty thousand people out of a population of seven hundred thousand were evacuated from Hanoi. The rest stayed to fight and to work. Provisional living places were built. The villagers who were not bombed helped the ones that were. People from other provinces who had already built their houses came here to build houses for the people in Hanoi. It was done very quickly.

Hanoi shot down more than three hundred and fifty American planes. Eight were shot down by the civilian forces. In the twelve days of bombing at Christmastime in 1972, Hanoi shot down thirty planes. We called it Dien Bien Phu in the air.

Grieving woman. Taken during the U.S. War.
COURTESY VIETNAMESE PHOTOGRAPHERS ASSOCIATION (TRAN CU).

Kham Thien Street, Hanoi

MRS. PHUNG THI TIEM

I AM THE HEAD of the Kham Thien Women's Union. I will tell you what happened. It was 10:20 on the evening of December 26, 1972. People had returned from work, eaten dinner, and many had already gone to bed. And then the Americans came. Many older people, women, men, and many children were killed in that bombing. They were supposed to have been evacuated, but the 24th was a Sunday and the 25th was Christmas Day. So people thought the Americans wouldn't bomb. They returned to their homes.

That evening buildings were destroyed, everything. Many people were injured and entire families were wiped out—from the youngest to the oldest. In one family, five generations were killed together, the baby inside its pregnant mother, the son, the mother, the grandmother and the great grandmother. Mrs. Xuan, who lives next door here, lost an arm. Five people were killed there. The woman on this monument over here, with the child, was the lady of the house. She took her children with her under the staircase, to protect them, and they were all killed. In one family there were nine children, and their parents died. Now they have grown up and left the neighborhood. Only the wounded ones are still here, working in shops. Families helped the wounded, and cooperatives and the Women's Union helped them, and continue to help them.

We spent that week digging out the shelters, looking for missing people. The smell of the dead was terrible. We collected the bodies in one place, and the wounded were taken to the hospital. People whose homes were bombed mostly went to live with relatives in the countryside.

American pilots dropped all those bombs, yet we were merciful. When an American pilot was shot down and brought through this very street, nobody touched him.

At the time, I was a factory worker. As head of the Women's Union of Kham Thien district, I had to set an example to the community, so I stayed, and my children had been evacuated. Only the workers could stay here, to work in the factories. Nobody in my family was killed.

Many people are handicapped today. Many people lost everything in the war, and can't support themselves. So you can tell the American government to make reparations. To be fair, the Vietnamese didn't send troops to invade America. Never, never forget. We remember the war. We remember our losses. All the little children—nine years old, thirteen, they had committed no crimes for the Americans to come and kill them. When they died in the bombings, their eyes popped out from the compression. Their bodies were mangled. Small children and old people. They lived here, and worked their whole lives here. They never sent troops to America. They never took one plant, one leaf from America. Why did the Americans come to destroy everything, to kill the people, to kill small children, to kill even pregnant women—why? Don't the American people even know why?

Nguyen Van Thong, with child. 1990. PHOTO BY M. HESS.

MR. NGUYEN VAN THONG

MY HOUSE IS AT 59 Kham Thien Street. They bombed at 10:42 in the evening. I was a volunteer youth, working on the Chuong Duong Bridge, and that night, when I passed the Thien Quang Lake on my way home, the planes came to bomb Hanoi. I got to my house and hesitated for a second outside, because I knew my father would scold me for being on the road during the bombing. At that moment a bomb dropped. I heard the noise and that was it. I went flying, and landed up by the next house.

My home was destroyed. I began to dig quickly, and found three bodies—my father, my younger brother, and my sister. My mother had been evacuated with the younger children. My older brother and sister-in-law I couldn't find. The next morning I found my brother's head. I never found my sister-in-law, nor one of my aunts. My uncle's body was found two months later, near the house. My neighbor Mr. Van, his wife and five children were killed, seven people.

In total, the Americans dropped three tons of bombs.

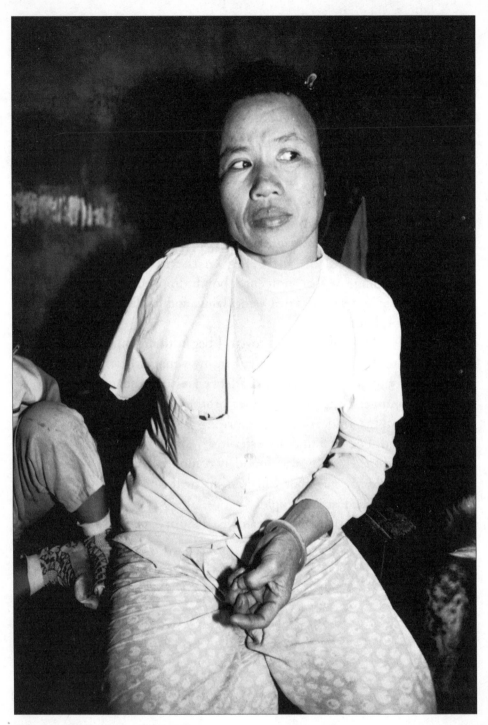

Nguyen Thi Xuan. 1990. PHOTO BY M. HESS.

MRS. NGUYEN THI XUAN

ON THE NIGHT of December 26, 1972, the Americans bombed the railway station and then they bombed right here. Just next door, where the monument now stands, a three-story house was destroyed. This two-story house here, three people were killed and two wounded, myself and this other woman here. In the next house four people were killed. In back of this house was bombed and many people were killed. My parents were killed, my grandmother, a niece and nephew. Five people in my family. There were only civilians living here on these streets. The B-52 planes bombed people, not military targets.

A piece of bomb cut my head and skull, and I lost my arm. I was taken to the hospital right away. Otherwise, I would be dead. After my mutilation, my husband left me and remarried. Now my brothers and sisters help me, because the government has little money for wounded civilians. I have pain all the time, here in my head, and my eyes keep tearing. I need an operation but it costs hundreds of thousands of *dong*. My life was destroyed by that bomb. Since then, it has no meaning.

Now there is peace, but why doesn't the American government pay? How can we live out our lives?

The Hanoi neighborhood of An Duong today. 1990. PHOTO BY M. HESS.

An Duong Neighborhood, Hanoi

*When we got out of the car with all my stuff,
an old woman said to Tuyen, "You came to take pictures
of what? They destroyed everything."*

MRS. TRAN THI DOI

FOUR PEOPLE were killed in my family, my husband, my two sons, and one daughter. I took their bodies to a village and asked the men there to bury them.

My house was completely destroyed. The reason I am alive is that I went to chat with a neighbor. My first daughter was coming from the hospital, and she was in the middle of the street when she saw the bombs, so she turned back. My youngest daughter went with me to the neighbor's house, so she is alive, too. They both have families now. I have remained here and keep my small shop.

You couldn't even find a rice bowl.

Nguyen Thi Ngo. 1990. PHOTO BY M. HESS.

MRS. NGUYEN THI NGO

I LOST ONE SON and my daughter-in-law in the 1972 bombing. She was pregnant. She was married to my first son, who suffered a head injury, and he's not right any more. They dug them out in the morning. The bomb dropped directly on this house, and then there was nothing.

DOCTOR TRAN QUOC DO
Bach Mai Hospital, Hanoi

I WAS ON DUTY at the time of the bombing in 1972. The American people have heard about the war and the bombing of Bach Mai Hospital from the radio, newpapers, television and films. But they can't picture everything that happened here, the suffering. In December 1972, the United States of America wanted to raze Hanoi to the ground, because they thought the Paris talks would then go more favorably. They bombed day and night. Families were evacuated but we stayed to work and fight. We took wounded people in for initial treatment, and then brought them to the evacuation center, where it was safer, but in fact it wasn't safe there either.

The B-52 planes sounded like the grinding of a rice mill. We saw the bombs drop and then the wounded started coming in. The bombs got closer and closer, and then they bombed us directly. We knew they were coming, and we brought the patients and the operating rooms underground. Under where you are now sitting are the shelters. We would do emergency treatment and then send the patients to a center in Hoa Binh, fifty, sixty kilometers from here. When the hospital was hit we were performing surgery underground and we didn't know. We came out and found half the buildings were destroyed. We have rebuilt them.

At that time my wife was working too, and we didn't dare evacuate our children. When they bombed An Duong, I saw children whose parents had died. They were brought to foster homes and the government cared for them. We decided to stay together in Hanoi. At least this way we would die together. Luckily, nothing happened to us.

We consider the American people our friends. We have gained freedom and unification. Now you can go out in our streets and say you are an American woman, and they respect you, and talk with you, and smile at you—everywhere, not only here. We don't hate and we don't think of vengeance. We remember the war, to keep peace.

Bach Mai Hospital after the Christmas bombing. 1972.
COURTESY OF THE WAR CRIMES MUSEUM IN HANOI.

We went to the Veterans Center in Hanoi
and sat around a table with a group of officers.

MR. PHU BANG

IT WAS REALLY two wars, the French and the American, and they cannot be separated. The Americans were already involved during the French War. Even the bombs were already being supplied by the United States. Secretary of State Dulles wanted to use the hydrogen bomb on Dien Bien Phu in 1954, but the British didn't agree to it.

I joined the army in 1945. I had no family life. I didn't see my mother for thirty years, until the liberation in 1975. She was in Saigon, and I was up here. I have to tell you, 1975 was a joyful time, when millions of young soldiers went to liberate South Vietnam.

You see, we had no communication with the South. A soldier would take a letter in his knapsack and carry it from Hanoi to Saigon on foot. This would take from three months to a year. I once received a letter from my wife after two years, and because it had been through rivers and rain and hot weather, I couldn't read it, the words were gone. I could only kiss her letter, I couldn't read it. The war was like that.

During *Mau Than*, the Tet Offensive, we were in the Cu Chi tunnels, near Saigon, together with women and children. I will never forget the children who were bombed in the shelters, the cries of the children we couldn't find.

I participated in the *Mau Than* attack on Ho Chi Minh City, and I was wounded in the head and legs. It was forty-five days before I got to a doctor. We were in the middle of the forest. There was no anesthesia. The doctor said, "Try not to cry." I still have the piece of shell he took out, from the Tropic Lightning 25th Division. The doctor brought over a beautiful assistant, and said, "Look at that beautiful face, Uncle, and don't cry."

Thousands of men went for years without ever seeing a woman. One time some women musicians came to perform for the troops at Dien Bien Phu. We made only one request. We said, "Beautiful girls, just stand there, so we can look at you."

But there were the soldiers from Nguyen Thi Dinh —that means the women soldiers. Mrs. Dinh is the head of the Women's Union. Her soldiers brought food and weapons to the army in the Long Mountains. They carried weapons and rice month after month, year after year.

What kind of life is that, this way of war?

We didn't start the war. Secretary of State Dulles and the U.S. government knew what the Geneva Agreements were, but they kept on bringing war matériel into Vietnam. They set up the puppet government of Ngo Dinh Diem, and built up and trained the soldiers of South Vietnam. Then they sent in their own troops. We had war for three generations.

MR. CHU

I WANT TO TELL you about the toxic chemicals and defoliants that were dropped on my unit. The first battle I took part in was the Johnson City Offensive, against American advisers, American weapons, and soldiers from South Vietnam. Because of their defeat, the Americans decided to drop toxic chemicals and defoliants over the highlands. We joined the battle in the Internal Province 5, as the area was called, in central Vietnam. We would attack and withdraw into the forest. Five days after dropping the toxic chemicals and defoliants, the forest was entirely burned. First the Americans used toxic chemicals to destroy the grass, and then they dropped napalm to burn the forest.

When our unit attacked Kon Tum town—an American headquarters was there—we liberated the district in one hour, and captured two American advisers. In retaliation, the Americans bombed for five days. After two days we withdrew. My most painful memory of this battle was that nine of my comrades were killed by toxic chemicals. When the bomb dropped, orange smoke rose up and burned the air. I buried nine of my comrades. They had no wounds, but their bodies had become smooth and soft.

The Americans had all kinds of chemical weapons. They just wanted to kill. We saw that in Chung Mai, when we had to retreat, and the American soldiers surrounded Kon Tum for two weeks. After two weeks, ten of

us were injured, eleven killed. That was in 1972. Most
had been killed by the toxic chemicals, and the injured
had been shot. The Americans knew we were still alive,
and they were using their toxic chemicals and defoliants
to kill everybody in Kon Tum. After a few days we had
just a little rice left, which we fed to the wounded. The
healthy soldiers went looking for the roots of banana
trees. We had no rice for ten days because we were surrounded by two American units and had only twenty-
seven people in the company. We decided to open the
road and move out. On a very rainy night we opened the
muddy road and carried out eleven dead and ten
wounded people. That was the worst time, being surrounded twenty days in the highlands, with the wind, the
rain, and the hunger.

LIEUTENANT-GENERAL LE THANH
General Secretary of the Vietnam Veterans Association

I JOINED THE revolution in 1943, fighting the Japanese, and then, in 1945, I participated in the general uprising. I fought the French, and later the Americans. I fought the Pako Division in 1975, and assisted in the Laos revolution. It was one long war and the consequences have been heavy, but the war is over and it is time to rebuild our country, rebuild our relations with other countries, and look to end all war.

They say we are difficult, that we won't help find the missing Americans. If there are seventeen hundred Americans missing, think how many missing Vietnamese there are after thirty years of war. In Vinh Linh, my comrade Mr. Lan says, how can one know who was killed, what day, what time, where? People don't know. In Vinh Linh, they buried people they didn't know. There were many, many graves. And the bombs came again, and we dug out the bodies and buried them again. And then the bombs came again. How could we find the families of the buried to tell them where their missing lie? But we are willing to help you find your Americans missing in action.

The American soldiers have gone to court because they, too, were affected by toxic chemicals and defoliants. Thousands and thousands of tons of toxic chemicals were dropped on my country, and what does the American government plan to do for Vietnam?

We can tell you many stories. We are victims and we are witnesses. We can tell you about our friends, ourselves, about what war feels like. Here is a simple story: My wife and I first fell in love in 1946, but because of the war we were separated and didn't marry until 1957. But from 1957 until now, I went from one battle to another. She would wait, and we would both count the days.

We don't want war. All the wars in Vietnam were brought upon us. We have a proverb: The tree wants to be still, but the wind won't let it.

Women soldiers by a downed U.S. plane. Taken during the U.S. War.
COURTESY VIETNAMESE PHOTOGRAPHERS ASSOCIATION (VAN BAO).

MRS. TRUONG MY HOA

Mrs. Hoa is a vice president of the Women's Union in Hanoi.

THE WAR ENDED fifteen years ago in victory for our people, but the country remains devastated. We say that victory cannot match our suffering. After all, the United States sent their troops over here with the intent to destroy all, burn all, and kill all. They destroyed the land.

In the South, the Americans burned villages and herded the women and children into camps surrounded by barbed wire. South Vietnam became an enormous prison. Many children couldn't go to school, people weren't free to work their land. They killed brutally, indiscriminately. You remember the massacre at My Lai, in Quang Ngai province. There were many other villages where the people were massacred. My Lai was only the worst.

Women everywhere were raped, killed, arrested, beaten. Pregnant women's bellies were cut open and their unborn babies thrown into burning houses. Thousands of women were imprisoned. Some were suspected V.C., some were real fighters, many were just ordinary people who were arrested and jailed for no reason. There were prisons all over the South. There were central prisons and provincial prisons and district prisons. Mothers with babies and pregnant women were arrested. They arrested old people and children and even handicapped people. I remember in Con Son prison there was an old blind woman, Mrs. Sau. She was kept in a tiger cage, with five or six people, all in a cage, covered by iron poles.

I was imprisoned in Con Son from 1964 to 1975. I had been a student in Ho Chi Minh City—Saigon at that time. I attended meetings and went to demonstrations to demand freedom and democracy. The South Vietnamese arrested me when I was nineteen, and I was thirty by the time I was released. All my family was active in the resistance for fifty years, and we each spent a long time in prison. My husband, too, spent fourteen years in jail, longer than me.

We were beaten and tortured. They had all kinds of sexual torture for the women.   And we were so hungry. When I was kept in the tiger cage at Con Son, I was given only a small tin of water and a little bowl of rice each day. There was a lot of sand, and when the winds blew, the sand covered our rice bowls. And flies, flies everywhere. Con Son was filthy and cold, a stone prison on a cold, windy island. We had one set of clothing a year. We never went outside, never bathed. We tore rags off our clothing for our menstrual periods, so that we were left with practically nothing to cover our bodies. There were all kinds of disease—dysentery, typhoid, cholera, malaria, small pox. Every morning we woke up wondering who had died in the night. There was no medicine. They said we could only have medicine if we would salute the South Vietnamese flag. We always refused. Many of my comrades died of disease, of hunger, of torture.

I spent a year in the tiger cage. On top they kept limestone and a water pot. If prisoners talked to each other they poured water and limestone over us, and if we cried they beat us with sticks, and then let the limestone burn our wounds. You can see right here, my forehead is scarred. They stuck sharp pins in my head. That was excruciating torture. I still have the scars. Many women never recovered.

The interrogators were always puppet troops. The Americans were the advisers. Sometimes they came there. We liked to say that the Americans had to change the color of their bodies. Too many of their soldiers were dying, so they had to use Vietnamese to kill Vietnamese.

Children in the South suffered terribly, and still suffer. They were left orphaned, with no homes, no food, no schools. They became beggars, dope dealers, thieves. We have orphans and widows and grieving mothers. We sing songs that tell the suffering of women who sent their sons to battle. And there are many women who never married because so many men in our country were killed. That's always the case in war. Whole families of women are left without men.

You must know about our "long-haired army" in Vietnam. The women operated on three fronts: political, military, and mobilization among the enemy troops. They were very effective in enemy territory. Women made great sacrifices. We know of mothers who suffocated their babies so they would not cry, in order to protect the troops. They sacrificed one life to save many.

Anti-aircraft gun. 1967.
COURTESY VIETNAMESE PHOTOGRAPHERS ASSOCIATION (TRAN CU).

Mother and daughter in their shop. 1990. PHOTO BY M. HESS.

Traveling West

In Moc Chau, a village in the highlands 210 kilometers
west of Hanoi, there is a monument to one hundred
and twenty-five people who were killed in a bombing raid
on June 14, 1965, at ten o'clock in the morning.

A mother in Muong Ang village, in the highlands between
Hanoi and Dien Bien Phu, remembered the war:

MY DAUGHTER was born right when the Americans were
bombing our village. I ran from the bombs into a thicket
of bamboo trees, and gave birth there. This is my
daughter.

Tuyen tells me, "The Vietnamese say, luck and happi-
ness come from a good mother."

Quyen drove us to Dien Bien Phu and back, over treacherous
mountain roads. He is a driver for the national tourist office,
Vietnamtourism. On one of his trips he met and married
a woman from Dien Bien Phu, and brought her back to
Hanoi. In 1979, during the two-month war with China,
he was drafted to bring weapons and troops to the border.
He is also a survivor of the U.S. bombing of Vinh. On the
road to Dien Bien Phu, he told me what he remembered.

MR. QUYEN

MY OLDEST SISTER was in a shelter when the bombs
dropped. They brought her out alive. That was in 1968,
and I was fourteen. We were in the suburbs, so we weren't
evacuated. They dropped all kinds of bombs, fragmentation bombs, napalm bombs, regular bombs. They
bombed the villages, the roads, and the rivers. They
bombed schools and hospitals. Our village was close to
Highway 1, the north-south road. They bombed that all
the time. We cooked underground. Once, in the fields, in
the middle of the afternoon, one of our school teachers
was cooking. The Americans saw the fire, and the whole
family was killed.

One time I saw a pilot get captured, but I didn't go
near him. I was afraid of getting bombed again. When an
American plane got shot down, the Americans would
bomb around the pilot, so that they could send in a helicopter to rescue him.

Vinh was a beautiful city before the war. Now there
is nothing left of what it was like. It used to be full of
trees, like Hanoi. Now there are no trees.

Dien Bien Phu

MR. NGUYEN HUU THIEN
a veteran of the French War

I AM NOT FROM HERE. My native land is south of
Hanoi. I was injured in the first attack on Dien Bien Phu,
and then I was injured again the second time. I got pieces
of shell in my skull and I was concussed from the bombs.
I thought I was dead. I was bleeding from my nose, my
eyes, my ears. A lot of people were killed at Dien Bien
Phu. One evening they brought in twelve people, one
small unit, and by morning there were two left. We didn't
even know each other's names.

After the war, my division went to rebuild Hoa
Binh, and then we were sent back to rebuild Dien Bien
Phu. I was in good health by then and knew the area well,
so I stayed. I retired as a soldier in 1959, and went to
work for the Internal Trade Department.

During the U.S. bombing, I was back and forth
between here and Lai Chu, a hundred kilometers away. I
used to go into the villages on the high mountain, seven
villages uphill, to buy lumber for the government. You
could only go at night, because it was close to the airport.
The planes were all over during the daytime. Nobody

lived here. They were all evacuated. There was no market, because people were afraid to congregate. We had oil lamps—we call them typhoon lamps—that we put on each side of the field. We would run the tractors from one side to the other. But we couldn't use the lamps because the planes would bomb right away.

It was terrible, because any plane on its way back from a bombing mission someplace else, to Haiphong, to Hanoi, would drop any bombs left over Dien Bien Phu, on the way back to Udon and Bangkok, in Thailand. For instance, if they saw smoke rising in a small village, or a couple of buffalos, they would bomb them. If people were on the road when the planes came, they had to lie down flat. The pilots bombed any moving targets. Once there was a man in a bamboo grove, and when they bombed it he was thrown high up into the bamboo, and he survived.

We rebuilt Dien Bien Phu after 1954. It was nice. There were lots of two-story houses. Now, for five kilometers, from one end of Dien Bien Phu to the other, there is nothing left. You can see that the old town center was destroyed. Everywhere they saw the red tile roofs of houses, they would drop bombs.

The villagers moved to the mountains. They dug shelters and tunnels, and then concealed them with earth. When they cooked at night, they covered their fires. Many people were killed because of the smoke from cooking. Even when they cooked in the forest, the smoke would signal a target for the American pilots, and they dropped their bombs, and people were killed.

If the villagers chose to work in the daytime, they went one by one or two by two, and only a few hours in the very early morning, before the fog lifted. Me too, if I had to go out on business, I would travel after 5:30 in the afternoon and until eight o'clock in the morning, when the fog lifted.

For our state shop, we built a tiny hut in the forest near the evacuation center and sold goods there, like salt and clothing. People continued to work, to produce, and even to earn a little money. Nobody stopped production. They used to say, "Stick to the fields, and fight." Most of the production was carried out by women, since the men were at the front. The Women's Union was very important during the war. They gave rice to the government and brought food to the soldiers around here.

Civilians stood outside the shelters with rifles and shot down airplanes. Years earlier, the troops at Dien Bien Phu had beat the French, and they were sure they would beat the Americans. During the French war, we had so very little, never enough weapons. We had guns made by the local people, a very primitive gun, and we had bamboo. But still we defeated the French. In the last fight we blew the buffalo horn, a terrrible sound. Traditionally in Vietnam, when bandits or the enemy came, they always blew the buffalo horn. The Vietnamese soldiers at Dien Bien Phu used it, too, to attack the enemy for the last fight. And so, the Vietnamese soldiers blew the horn and the French drew up the white flag to surrender. When the Americans came with their bombs, we believed we would defeat them too.

All around here you can see land scars. The craters were made into fish ponds. There's one right here.

MR. CAO TIEN DUNG

THE AMERICANS started bombing here on July 2, 1965. They continued bombing for four days. I was a store-keeper then, and I had to be evacuated. They bombed and shot rockets for a month, and eventually destroyed Dien Bien Phu. One day in 1965, at six o'clock in the morning—it was in the winter—a group of reconnais-sance planes flew overhead, and dropped two tons of bombs. A woman and child were killed. You can still see the crater. My children and I were inside our house. If it weren't for the bamboo here, we would be dead. We rebuilt the house in 1975.

It was difficult to farm, and the rice fields suffered. But the women were united and worked the land. Their husbands and children were at the front and so they worked the land. A woman's life is always more difficult than a man's. Here, of course, but maybe everywhere.

That was the first round. As it became clear that they were being defeated, the Americans became even more barbarous, more vengeful. They bombed everything. They behaved like a beast in the forest. When an animal is wounded, while it is dying, it can be terrible and will attack everything and everyone around it. The way I see it, in South Vietnam the puppet government changed many times, and it was always unstable. The North Vietnamese fought very well, and the Americans were get-ting weaker and weaker in the South. So they bombed the North, in order to destroy the economy and keep our sol-diers from moving south.

I have been retired for a long time and I don't know much about the war, but I believe that this brutality was the Americans' revenge. Their weakness was beginning to show. If they wanted to be strong, they should have done something bigger, but they got mean with the enemy when they were losing.

I fought the French here in 1954, with the 316th Division, and I stayed on after the war. Now I am retired. I work in my garden, and I teach children. Five brothers in my family went to the front. Peace came, and all five returned. So we were very lucky.

We visited a Kang village near Dien Bien Phu. The Kang are
a Thai people. We were taken to Mr. Hac's home, a bamboo
house in the middle of a cornfield, high up on stilts, with
animals living underneath. It was one huge room, a wood
fire at one end and food cooking. Women sat around the fire.
Our group joined the men at the other end. Since Mr. Hac
speaks a Thai dialect, somebody translated into Vietnamese
for Tuyen, who in turn translated into English for me. It was
so remote and so difficult to get to and so far from home, I
wondered what they could tell me about America.

MR. LO VAN HAC

THIS WHOLE VILLAGE burned, about thirty-five families.
When they spotted houses, the Americans bombed them.
The farms were all destroyed. The planes came through
Laos in 1964, and over our village. I have a piece of rocket
in my skull, on the side. They took a large cloth to ban-
dage the wound, but I couldn't stop bleeding.

ANOTHER VILLAGER

HE IS DEAF from the bombing, and he suffered concussion injuries.

The Americans wanted to destroy the roads, in order to stop the trucks from going to Laos. The planes came here and saw the villages, and they shot off their rockets and bombs. First they dropped the bombs and then they shot rockets into the villages, so that the villages burned. Planes came in groups of four. Two came to drop bombs, went back up, and then the other two came down and dropped bombs. Then the first two returned to shoot the rockets, went back up, and the second two came. It was the same thing in the French War. They dropped bombs and shelled. We thought it was all the same war. And the Japanese came here, too, to shoot and bomb. In 1952, the French came down in parachutes, and the Viet Minh came, and they beat the French. Then the Americans came.

Lo Van Gion, with some of his family. 1990. PHOTO BY M. HESS.

MR. LO VAN GION

THE FRENCH PARACHUTED into the Dien Bien Phu plateau on November 20, 1953, at nine o'clock in the morning, and rounded up all the families over by Muong Thanh, the French military base. Eventually, everybody was collected into one village, Lung Nhai. There were more than ten thousand people. They destroyed our houses, took the wood, and used us to build shelters, roads, whatever they wanted.

By April 25, 1954, the road from Muong Thanh to Hon Kum was already cut off. The French thought the Viet Minh were in our village, so they bombed it. There were actually no soldiers living there, just some traitors who wanted money, who would point at whomever and say they were Viet Minh. People who worked for the French got a lot of money, and salt. Later, we caught them.

There was a plane with no tail, two wings. It rises up and all the bombs come down. Mostly it dropped napalm, and people burned to death. After bombing, they shelled the village. Four hundred and forty-four people were killed, all Thai, no Vietnamese. At four o'clock in the afternoon they bombed Lung Nhai, and it burned for three days. Everywhere there were dead people, cows, buffalos, pigs, dogs. Some people died later, two, three weeks later, after suffering wretched burns. There was no hospital, no doctors. On the fourth day we began to look for the missing among the dead, and we couldn't tell who was who. There was nothing left. Rice, clothing, blankets, everything was burned. The suffering was terrible. I saw a girl standing beside her dead mother, and a dog came to eat the dead body, and people came and beat the dog. I remember that. I can't describe it. The people bowed their heads and wept. Later, soldiers came and buried the bodies in one day.

The French never paid us anything, and they said nothing.

After the battle of Dien Bien Phu, we hoped the war was over. From 1954 to 1964, we rebuilt our villages and the city. We built a school and a hospital. Life was good, peaceful, quiet, until Johnson and Nixon launched the escalation war and destroyed North Vietnam. How can I explain to you the suffering of war? In the daytime we went to the forest, and came back at night to work in the fields. Houses and villages of the Thai people, like this one, were destroyed. My father's house was twice as big as this, and it was destroyed by bombs. The American War lasted a very long time. They bombed and shelled and shot rockets in 1964, 1965, 1966, 1967, 1968, and 1972. Mostly they bombed civilian and economic targets. There were no military forces here.

Dien Bien Phu was much bigger before. They are still rebuilding, but there is no money. The hospital has been rebuilt, but it was much bigger before. It has taken more than ten years of building. Our economy has suffered because of the war with China, because of the embargoes of America and China, because of bad weather. My request: That the international community help the Vietnamese. Especially the Americans should help to rebuild Dien Bien Phu. They caused so much suffering, how can we forget? I don't think the American people wanted their husbands and sons shot and killed in Vietnam.

MR. PHAM VAN HUNG

WHEN WE CELEBRATED the tenth anniversary of the victory of Dien Bien Phu in 1964, the village was once again beautiful, even my school. But the Americans didn't leave a roof tile intact. Even the smallest bridge over a tiny stream had been bombed over and over.

At that time we ate corn and manioc. Now we feed it to the pigs. Then, the rice was mostly reserved for the soldiers, though many stores of rice were burned.

I was fifteen when the Americans bombed my school, on April 10, 1967, at seven o'clock in the morning. We heard the gong, and the teachers took us to the shelters. After the planes left, we were taken to the forest, to safety. The school was all smoke and flames, but we were safe. The teacher that had beat the gong didn't get to the shelter on time. There was another teacher who had borne a child just nine days before and couldn't run. They were both killed. The baby was raised by his father until he was nine years old, when he drowned in the river. Once, five people were killed in a shelter and three children lost their parents. One of them was my classmate. The townspeople donated money to these children. One joined the army, one became an engineer, and the third became a doctor. I became a teacher, and now I am deputy director of my old school.

The Americans committed such crimes against the Vietnamese people, but we want to be friends. On this earth, on this planet, I want only smiles and song.

SOUTH

OF THE

17TH

PARALLEL

Tran Van Nhan's mother-in-law. 1991. PHOTO BY M. HESS.
OVERLEAF: Military cemetary opposite the old American base at Chu Lai.
1990. PHOTO BY M. HESS.

Tay Ninh

MR. TRAN VAN NHAN

TAY NINH USED TO BE dense forest. The Americans came with bulldozers and toxic chemicals and defoliants, and they destroyed it.

In 1945 I joined the youth forces. I fought the French and the Americans right here in my native land. After the Geneva Agreement we were supposed to go to North Vietnam. I stayed underground. In the daytime I lived as a farmer, at night I carried a gun. We killed Ngo Dinh Diem's men. Later the Americans came, and we went into the tunnels. First they came to Cu Chi—we are close to Cu Chi. They had tanks two hundred meters from my house, to block the road to Saigon. By then I was head of the battalion, and I fought them here in An Tinh. That's a famous battle. Three hundred American soldiers were killed.

My brother was killed. He had survived prison at Con Son and had come back here, until they found him in a secret tunnel. A lot of people switched sides, joined the puppet forces—we call them *chieu hoi*—but they never betrayed my wife. A concentration camp existed here, and my family lived in it. If you wanted to leave you had to get permission, and when you returned you had to tell them you were back. The American and puppet soldiers were terrible. When they captured people, they tied them by the neck and dragged them behind their tanks, and then they cut off their heads. Many women were raped, but they never talk about it.

Mr. Nhan's eighty-two-year-old mother-in-law sat in on this conversation, along with various members of his enormous family—he has nine children. She said that she lived here through the occupation by the French and the Japanese and the Americans, who were very big and tall.

MR. THE NGOC PHAN

We stopped in the village of Trang Bang, in Tay Ninh province, at the place where nine-year-old Kim Phuc was photographed running down the road, naked and screaming from a napalm hit. This is her brother.

I AM THE THIRD CHILD, Kim Phuc is the sixth. Everyone in our family was struck by the bomb. Two children were killed right away, and Kim Phuc was burned. It was June 4, 1972. The houses had been bombed many times before, but that time we were hit by napalm. They had been bombing for a month. We called it the Battle of Pouring Fire. We had been living in tunnels with only the clothes on our back. And when they told us we had to go to an evacuation center we came out, and that's when they dropped the napalm. We were all burned. At first we couldn't find Kim Phuc. We buried the two children and went to look for her. Three days later we found her at the hospital in Ho Chi Minh City. They had put her with the dead bodies, and later saw she was still breathing. She looked like she was dead, with all her flesh burned off. She cried all the time, it was so painful. From 1972 until 1984 her skin continued to burn, twelve years. Then a journalist came and brought her to Germany for treatment. She is studying medicine in Cuba now.

Cu Chi, near Ho Chi Minh City

MR. VU

THESE SCARS ARE FROM NAPALM. I was a soldier in the Liberation Forces in Cu Chi. I lived in the tunnels from 1968 to 1975. We came out to fight. There was enough food in the tunnels to last a year. At night we could go into the villages. During Tet, the New Year, we celebrated with villagers, who would bring us food and supplies. Sometimes these people were caught. They were beaten, tortured, and imprisoned, but they never gave us away.

From 1968 to 1970 my family lived in the concentration camp at Trung Lop. The American and puppet armies wanted to build a training base here, and so everybody was brought to the concentration camps in Trung Lop or Tay Ninh, or elsewhere. The armies brought in bulldozers and dropped defoliants and razed our land. Everything was burned, wiped out, and became a desert. You can see since liberation some growth, but before the war there were big trees and the land was rich and fertile. You can still find roots of bamboo and fruit trees.

MR. BIEN VAN DON

I LOST MY LEGS when I was only fifteen. I was out watching the buffalos, and I stepped on a mine. Our parents were already dead, and so my brothers and sisters were looking after one another. They kept us in the concentration camp at Trung Lop. Those black and white Americans were tall and big, different. You had to ask permission to come and go. I was small, and didn't go outside the camp. In 1970, the Liberation Forces attacked the military post and destroyed the camp, and the people went back to their villages.

After a year in the hospital, I came back here to live with my sister. The battles were at night. I would go down on my hands by the entrance of the tunnel, and when the fighting started I would roll inside. They dropped napalm and other kinds of bombs, and turned the forests into a white desert.

Now I watch that the ducks and chickens don't come into my family's house. I don't have a normal life like other people. Without legs, I stay in one place.

MR. TRAN VAN DEM

I AM SIXTY-ONE, according to the moon calendar. According to the solar calendar, I am sixty-two. I was working in the fields when an American mine exploded, and I lost my eyes. We were kept in concentration camps. They let us out to work, but we had to get permission every day.

Before the war we had clothing and food, more than enough food to eat. Maybe if we had the technology, we could recover our rich economy. Many, many people here have no arms, no legs—war wounded. I remember all kinds of bombs—napalm bombs, petrol bombs, powder bombs. All kinds of bombs fell here.

Nguyen Thi Sam. 1991. PHOTO BY M. HESS.

MRS. NGUYEN THI SAM

I WAS WOUNDED BY BOMBS in 1969, in the legs, lost this arm, lost my hearing, and in my right eye I can't see. I do my best. My husband was killed by bombs the year before, in *Mau Than*. We had five children. They survived the war, and now I have grandchildren. They help, and sometimes the government gives me money and rice.

They put us in a concentration camp. Before they came, they always dropped bombs. Then they launched the mopping-up operations. Sometimes there was fighting and they would shell back and forth. Other times they just shot randomly. We stayed in the tunnels. Many people here were killed by bombs and shelling. They used powder bombs and napalm bombs, and they took bulldozers and turned the land and our homes into a desert.

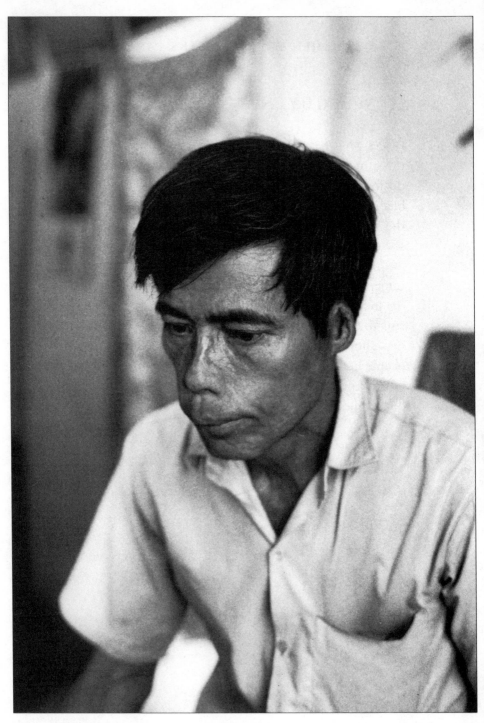

Phan Van Chinh. 1991. PHOTO BY M. HESS.

MR. PHAN VAN CHINH

I WAS BORN IN THIS VILLAGE in 1947. At the end of 1965, the Americans came in helicopters and destroyed the villages to build a huge military base. They used napalm to clear the land. The people who could run, ran. I was burned by napalm and lost consciousness, so I don't remember very much. Later on I felt terrible pain. All my skin came off. Every part that can burn was burned. I was taken to the hospital in Saigon. Whenever the doctors changed the bandages I was made to turn, and this caused terrible pain. When I came back the houses were gone, burned. And so we went to the camp in Tan Thong to live. I stayed there ten years, until 1975. I am a little bit deaf now, and, worse than that, my eyes cannot see far or very clearly.

Huynh Phuong Anh. 1990. PHOTO BY M. HESS.

Nha Trang City

MRS. HUYNH PHUONG ANH

MY NATIVE HOME IS HERE in Nha Trang, but when I was eight years old I was evacuated to the North with my parents, in 1954. This was when Vietnam was divided between the North and the South. In 1968 I went south with the Liberation Forces, to fight in the mountains. Nobody had enough rice. We had no meat, no fish, only salt with rice. I had malaria, the kind you get in the mountains, and nearly died from it. The Americans parachuted soldiers in for mopping-up operations, and when we would pass through villages where they had been, we would find only bodies—in the trees, on the ground, and women with cloth stuffed in their mouths. The people were gone, only wounded and the dead. You see, when the Americans came through they killed everyone, even children, because they thought they were V.C.—Viet Cong.

In 1971 I was wounded. We had U.S. dollars sent down from the North that we converted to piasters, and we would come down from the mountains to the villages to buy rice. One time the Americans recognized us, and I was shot. The bag of rice protected me, but a piece entered my side here. I went back north, and in 1973 I married. We had waited nine years to get married, because he was in the South, too, fighting the war.

After the war I developed uterine cancer, and two years ago I had to have surgery. My sister too. When we lived in the forest, the U.S. planes had dropped thousands of gallons of defoliant. In the hospital there were many women who had this form of cancer, and they too had lived in contaminated areas.

Sa Huynh Village

MRS. QUI

DURING THE WAR my village was burned so many times by the Americans that we went to live in the mountains. They bombed there too, and we came here. All the villages were bombed, and many, many people were killed. If we got to a shelter, we lived. I had eight children, and two of them were killed by bombs, two more died from sickness. We tried to buy medicine in the market, but the American and South Vietnamese forces wouldn't let us go there. They thought we were bringing something to the Viet Cong. Two of my children died because they had no medicine.

During the war with the French, I was still very young, and we lived in the plains, not the mountains. In the second war, with Diem and the Americans, we were captured, beaten, and we were helpless when our homes were set on fire. Bombs and bullets, killing and death. How can we not hate the Americans?

Mrs. Qui. 1990. PHOTO BY M. HESS.

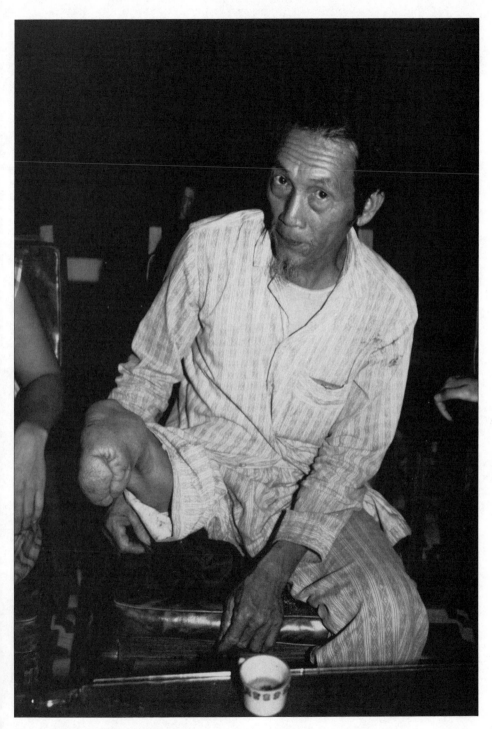

Trinh Thap. 1990. PHOTO BY M. HESS.

MR. TRINH THAP

I AM 66 YEARS OLD. In 1965 or 1966—I forget which—
the Americans were shelling from the sea, here, into the
village. While I was taking wood down to save my
burning house, I got hit. I was a civilian—a farmer, but
now I can't work. I must live off my wife and children.
The villagers donated money for me to buy this artificial
leg. Whenever the rubber cushion wears out, I make
another myself, because I have no money to buy new
ones.

The whole village was destroyed by the bombs and
the shelling, the houses, even the palm trees. The farmers
couldn't work because they had to stay underground, in
the shelters. We had ten hectares of land but we could
only work two. We could work near the road where it was
easy to get to the shelter, but we had to leave the land up
the mountain. We had no breakfast, no lunch, only
dinner. Sometimes we had a good meal, sometimes we
had nothing.

We were farmers, and we didn't know why the
Americans were shelling us.

Quang Ngai Province

MRS. BACH THI LAN

I WAS BORN in the Son Tinh district of Quang Ngai province, where My Lai used to be. When I was fourteen, our village was liberated and I started to work for the provisional district committee, in the youth office. I did things like carry messages. As I was the eldest daughter, a strong hand for the field, my family made a great sacrifice when they encouraged me to work for the revolutionary committee. After Mau Than, in 1968, I transferred to the transportation division of the volunteer forces and worked on the roads.

I was directly exposed to American defoliants four times. I have had two miscarriages and my liver is enlarged. And malaria, of course, everyone in Vietnam had it. In 1971, the Americans attacked the road I was working on, and I got shot in the leg. You can see, one is shorter than the other. I was twenty-one years old, very young. I still feel pain. After that, I couldn't work on the roads, so I took a training course in pharmaceuticals and began to work in a clinic for the transportation division.

I got married after the liberation and now have four children. Women always said it was better to wait until liberation to get married. The war was more difficult for women than for men but our duty was the same, to liberate the country. We were equal. I can't say that I was never afraid, but the Vietnamese people were suffering. In my own family I lost my brother and an uncle, and my father was beaten by Americans in a village operation. So, though I joined the war at the beginning of my life, I have never regretted it.

This is the first time I have met you, and I can see that you are a woman like me, and you can talk with me, and want to understand my life. You are an American and I am Vietnamese. As women we can talk.

DOCTOR KY

THE WORST FIGHTING in the war for South Vietnam was when the American troops arrived. When they first came here to Quang Ngai province, they killed everyone in our clinic—doctors, assistants, and the wounded soldiers, too. I escaped. We had seven doctors and assistants working there. Before the troops arrived, the American advisers and puppet soldiers dropped bombs so parachute soldiers could land, but they didn't find us then.

Today—right now there is a man in our hospital who recently stepped on a mine left over from the American time. In 1989, about five people were injured from exploding mines, just in this district. Sometimes when farmers plow the land close to the old American camps they step on live mines. There were also a lot of toxic chemicals dropped in this area, and many women have had deformed babies. Last year we had three children with leukemia. So people are still getting hurt from the war. We have nothing here, no money for the hospital. Mostly we lack medicine. During the war we got a lot of medicine from the North, and we even bought medicine in Saigon, used American medicine to treat soldiers from the Liberation Forces.

My Lai

MRS. HA THI QUI

IN THE EARLY MORNING, just after we got up, the helicopters came and started shelling, and soldiers poured out onto the fields. I was eating breakfast. We thought it might be like the other times the Americans came into the village. They gave the children candy. Or like the second time, when Americans came to take water from the well to fill their canteens, and then left, and they didn't do any harm to the people. But the third time, March 16, 1968, when they came to the hamlet they rounded up all the people. Some they took to the roadside and shot right away. The people on the guard tower were all killed. And some they brought over to this ditch, here. First they shot Mr. Cau. He was a monk. He lived in the pagoda. Then they forced everyone into the ditch and shot them. I was wounded in the backside. At first I felt very, very hot, and later on very cold. And they killed—you see, they fired a first time into the ditch, and many men, children and women were killed. They cried, "Mother." They were screaming. The soldiers fired three more times and finished the cries of the people. The first time there were still people screaming. They fired a second time, and the third time it was finished, all the people were killed.

129

Afterwards, I got up to go back to my house, and I saw nothing. All the houses had been burned. They had cut down our village tree by the pond. They had cut all the trees down in the orchards. They had killed everyone. There were dead bodies all over the village. I took a little dead baby back to the house from the roadside. It was my daughter's child.

I went to the next hamlet and found my younger sister-in-law killed, lying on the floor. And I found her daughter's body, a fifteen-year-old girl, all her clothing torn off and her legs were spread open—raped by Americans.

They had no mercy, the Americans. You see, they had come here many times and we got along with them. Then they came and killed all the people. They showed no mercy for the people. We had done nothing to them. If they had killed people at the beginning, one or two, we would have known to run, but we didn't know.

I went back to my house and there was nothing, not even a pair of trousers to wear, because everything had been burned. The houses kept on burning, and I couldn't find anyone. I went to another hamlet, untouched by the Americans, to get food and clothing, and told them what had happened at Son My, and they came and carried the dead people away. There was a terrible smell.

My oldest daughter was killed. You bear a child and bring her up, and then she gets killed. My husband had gone to work in the fields very early, so he escaped. Twice before, the Americans had come here and done nothing. We don't understand why the third time they killed the people.

After 1968 we were rounded up and moved to a camp about three, four kilometers from here. The Americans surrounded the camp and we lived inside.

The Americans had lived alongside the Vietnamese people, and we did nothing to them. We worked, spent all our lives in the fields. How could they come and kill us that way? So we are very sad about the massacre, full of sorrow, the village people and the farmers, very sad about it.

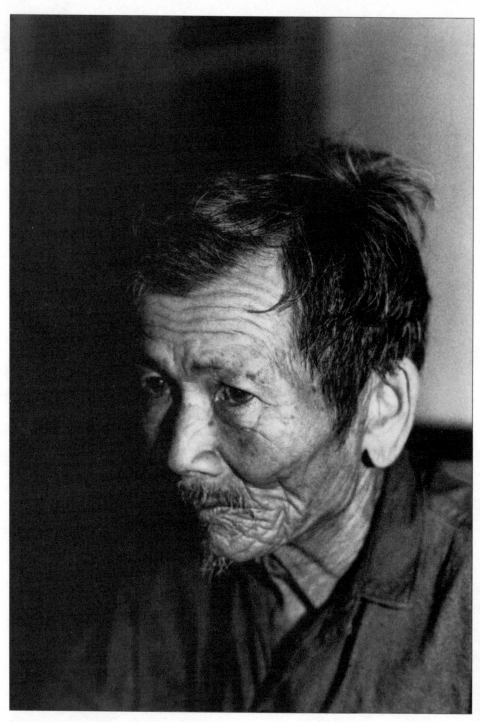

Pham Dong. 1991. PHOTO BY M. HESS.

MR. PHAM DONG

MOST OF US WERE JUST RISING. We saw many, many helicopters coming toward us and around the village. You could see helicopters in all four directions. We were calm, I don't know why. Then the Americans started shelling from the helicopters, and then the soldiers ran out onto the fields. They came from all directions, and we didn't know where to run.

The first group of Americans came in and shot the people, and they killed the buffalos and cows. They shot everyone they saw, even pregnant women and old people. They shot everyone. The second group came and burned the houses, cut down the trees, all the fruit trees.

There was an old man, about seventy or eighty years old. The soldiers cut off his hand and threw it to the ground, and then they threw him into the well and shot him. After that, most of the people were rounded up and brought to the ditch here. The Americans pushed them into the ditch and then they shot them. They didn't care who—old people, children, pregnant women too. They killed them all. I myself saw this massacre. I was very lucky to survive. When I fell into the ditch I landed close to the edge. I saw people being killed, and I took a cloth from somewhere and covered my head, and pretended to die.

My whole family was killed. When it seemed as if they had stopped shooting, my child got up and called out to me. He looked around the ditch. An American shot him through the heart. My wife and child, they shot my wife and child.

They went away and then came back, to see if there were any survivors, and they kept on killing. Some tried to run, and they shot them to death.

My brother, his wife and their three children were killed, five in all.

After the Americans left we ran. In the evening we came back to bury the people. The Americans never came back, because, you see, they had killed everyone, so why come back here, for what? They went on to other villages. They had suffered big losses, the Americans, so because of that they were angry.

MR. TINH

I WAS BORN AND RAISED HERE in Son My. First the South Vietnamese forces arrived from Saigon, and then the Americans came directly. They killed many people in their mopping-up operations, and then destroyed the homes and villages. When I witnessed this myself, I decided to take up arms. I was a guerrilla from 1970 to 1975. When the tanks came, we would come up from the tunnels to fight. I got wounded on the foot here, and my hand. Pieces from a shell cut my hand and I lost four fingers. When the weather changes, my wounds still bother me.

This place was made barren. There were no more trees, nothing left in the earth. Petrol bombs and bitter-smelling bombs, that made you taste something very bitter, had destroyed everything. My family, our buffalos, all our animals were killed. My comrades and I grew up hating the Americans, and we took up arms to fight them. Many were sacrificed in battle, but we never thought we would be defeated. Our only thought was to fight and to win.

OVERLEAF: An abandoned American gas station in the Mekong Delta. 1991.
PHOTO BY M. HESS.

Quang Nam Danang Province

On the road just south of Danang, we stopped to talk with a group of women who had lived through the American occupation. The following two did most of the talking.

MRS. NGUYEN THI HUONG

THE AMERICANS WERE EVERYWHERE. They put us on Dinh Chi Island—over there—to live. During the day we went to the mountains, where the Liberation Forces were, and came back at night. We were afraid of the Americans, so we stayed away in the daytime. They figured that if we live here we must be V.C. And so when they lost their men in operations, they came to our villages to beat and torture us, even children. Most of our men were gone. There were only women and children and old people.

MRS. DANG THI SINH

I WAS TORTURED AND BEATEN, beaten a lot. Once, I brought some things to the market to sell, and because an American had been shot by guerrillas, they took me and beat me. They kept me for ten days at the Danang airport, and then they let me go—because I had nothing to tell. That was the worst time, when I was tortured for ten days. One man asked me, in the American language, to look at him, but instead I looked at the interpreter, and right away this man kicked me—for not looking at him in the face.

The Americans wore big jackets, flak jackets, and they looked very, very big. They raped many young girls. We all have family that were killed by the Americans.

When they thought an area belonged to the V.C., they would round up the people and take away the suspects. So when they came, we ran. And when they returned to their base we went back to the fields. Sometimes, after a night of shelling, we brought the dead and wounded to the base, to protest and demand compensation. We asked for rice. They burned our houses and then they brought us rice. And they gave us tin, to build new houses.

Marble Mountain is outside of Danang, right next to what the Americans called China Beach. I met these three people in a shop that makes and sells sculptures of local marble.

MRS. HUYNH THI TRINH

IN MY VILLAGE on the other side of the bridge, the Americans had mopping-up operations every day, so we came here to live. They were always shelling. They were always looking for V.C. They would point at people, and when we ran, we were shot. Sometimes we were caught and then shot.

MR. HUYNH PHUOC TINH
21 years old, recounts stories he heard while growing up.

THERE IS ONE WOMAN here, Mrs. Dung, whose breasts were cut off by the Americans. Now she is crazy. They forced her to drink some kind of medicine, to tell where the V.C. were, but she didn't tell anything. They beat her, tortured her, and they cut off her breasts.

One time an American was killed. And they burned down the entire village and killed many people, for revenge. Our house was burned. My father told me about it. My father was in the Liberation Forces, and he was caught and spent some years in prison.

MR. HUYNH PHUOC CHON
Tinh's father

I STARTED FIGHTING IN 1955, against the South Vietnam government of Ngo Dinh Diem, and then against the Americans from 1965. I was betrayed and arrested in 1970. First they put me in jail at Hoi An. I was tortured innumerable times, by South Vietnamese soldiers and then by Americans. First I was beaten. Then they threw me to the ground and jumped on my chest. I said nothing. So they took me to the base and they continued to torture me. Then they brought me someplace else and tortured me some more. First the South Vietnamese and then the Americans tortured me. They had me in a very small room, like this, where they put electricity on my fingertips. They beat me and beat me until I lost consciousness, and then they beat me again, because they could get no information. I was tortured for four, five months. They brought me to Thanh Loc, also in Danang province, and then to the police station, and then back to the jail. All that time they tortured and interrogated me. I have never regained my health. Finally I was taken to Con Son Island. It was built by the French and enlarged during the American time. I would go sometimes five, six days without food, and nothing to drink. For one month I didn't move I was so sick. I was released in 1973, after the Paris Agreements. Now I am a farmer.

Luu Thi Nao. 1991. PHOTO BY M. HESS.

MRS. LUU THI NAO

THEY PUT EVERYBODY in a camp. If we tried to stay in our village they burned the houses. If we still stayed, they shelled the villages and destroyed them. But we would escape from the camp and come back home. The camp was terrible—very bad conditions. It was not just the lack of things, but the lack of freedom. You see, there were not only American and South Vietnamese soldiers but also South Korean, and they were barbarous. They raped the women. They had a list of people suspected of belonging to the V.C. and I was on it. For a few months I was put in prison. They thought that maybe I helped the V.C., something like that, and they arrested me. They beat me. I had nothing to eat, no water. There was nothing.

I had two sons that were killed in battle, and my husband was killed too.

It was a very bad life.

MRS. NGUYEN THI DUC

Mrs. Nguyen Thi Duc works in a little canteen at the Pacific Hotel in Danang, where we were staying. She is thirty-two now. I asked her what she remembers of the occupation.

THE SOUTH KOREANS were especially brutal. They raped the women and girls in our village. In 1965, my aunt was raped. They cut off her hands and legs, and threw her in the river.

We were rounded up into areas controlled by American and South Vietnamese soldiers. The old ones didn't want to go, and so the soldiers would tie ropes around their necks and drag them. My uncle was killed like that, being dragged by the neck. They burned all the houses. We were given very little food. There was no school. We were kept in the camps for ten years, until 1975.

Dien Duong Village

MR. LE VAN KY

THE AMERICANS OCCUPIED Danang in 1966. They came in tanks. At first the guerrillas fought them, but by the end of the year they had destroyed the land with bombs. Mopping-up operations lasted until 1969. The South Korean Green Dragon brigade base was between here and the airport. Most of the people were kept at Cam Ha and Thanh Thuy, the concentration camps, including my family, and I stayed here to fight. I was in command of the local guerrillas. My wife was arrested many times, beaten, tortured, and spent six years in prison. Villagers looked after our children. In 1967, the Americans and South Koreans killed thirty-four people in one hamlet, forty people in another, seven people here. In one day they killed 140 people in Dien Duong. When they came to destroy the crops, the people used whatever they had—tree branches, sticks—to beat off the soldiers. At that point they would be shot. The Americans and South Koreans raped women. They put them in houses and set the houses on fire. After the massacres, we buried the dead.

MR. LE NGOC DUONG

IN 1965, HERE IN DIEN DUONG, we captured the first American soldier in the South. We called him Bobby. I was a guerrilla at the time.

Dien Duong was a liberated zone. The American coalition had terrorized the people into leaving so that they wouldn't be able to help the Liberation Forces. Very few people betrayed us. That's why the Americans killed civilians. Entire families were wiped out, with no one left to put perfume sticks on their ancestral tables.

Civilians were put in concentration camps. The Americans bombed and shelled and destroyed the land with chemicals, and then soldiers came in and killed the remaining people. There was a South Korean military post about one kilometer away, on the sea. The South Koreans helped the Americans. In February 1968, they took twenty-five or thirty women, children and older people. They put them in houses a couple of hundred meters from the post, poured gasoline over the houses, and burned them down. The people that ran out were shot. When they didn't return we went, at night, and found them there. That was the first of three massacres. The second time was similar. They rounded up the people about five hundred meters from where we are sitting. All the houses connected to a tunnel to enable people to escape the shelling and bombs. Six people were put in one of these shelters, shot, and then burned. The third massacre, people were collected from one village and the

South Koreans came with tanks and began firing. Then they buried the bodies and razed the village. One hundred and twenty people were killed.

At night nobody was permitted to leave the camps. In the daytime, if the soldiers didn't think the people were going to help the Viet Cong, they let them go to the fields, to grow rice, potato, manioc.

Vietnamese lives were wretched. I cannot describe it all for you, the difficult days in this land. By 1969 there was nobody left, only guerrillas and local forces. The civilians had moved on to the city, to Danang and Hoi An, and other places.

We had no weapons. The Americans and their coalition had very modern weapons—simple against modern, so we had to be clever. They didn't know that the V.C. surrounded their camps. We took unexploded bombs and shells, and made mines. We put them on the roads and destroyed their tanks. We saw where they were coming from and we mined those places. There was a hill northeast of here which overlooked the village, where they camped. We made a huge mine, took a 200-liter can of petrol, filled it with explosives, connected it to a line and planted it on that hill. I was one kilometer away, so there was no sound at first. We saw a lot of smoke and American bodies flying in the air, and then we heard the explosion. Helicopters came and removed the bodies, but they left one. We bound him in cloth and buried him. Alive they were our enemies, but in death we were all human. The Americans came back with tanks and trucks, and now we can't find his grave.

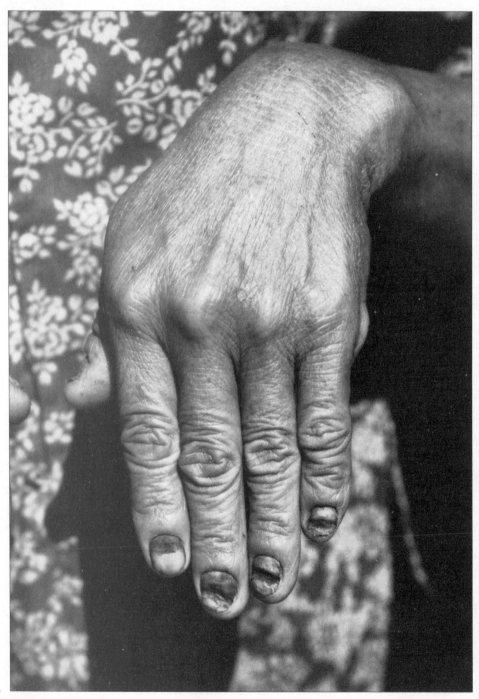

Le Thi Dieu's fingernails are dead and broken, 25 years after torture by American soldiers. 1991. PHOTO BY M. HESS.

MRS. LE THI DIEU

IN 1965 I WAS ARRESTED by the Americans and brought to Hoi An. They put electricity in my vagina, on my nipples, in my ears, in my nose, on my fingers. Blood came out of my vagina. At night they put electricity inside my body and they beat me. They jumped on me with their shoes. Now when I breathe my whole chest hurts, and when I lie on the bed my body aches. They kept me for eighteen months.

In 1967 I was arrested again. They brought me to the center of the village and tied me up, both hands in back, like this. They poured soapy water down my throat all night. My face and chest and belly swelled up and I lost consciousness. They took me to the base, and there they beat me and again put electricity on my body. They poured water mixed with hot peppers down my throat. I thought I had already died. Then they took me to the hospital. I stayed there a week. When they brought me back to the base, they beat me again, gave me more electricity. They tortured me for information but they got nothing. They poured water down my throat again, and I stopped breathing.

They took me to a little house, like this, and one American tried to rape me. I started screaming, and he took my hair, which was very long, and he dragged me and beat me. A Vietnamese interpreter came and said, "Why do you struggle against the Americans? It won't do any good." And I said, "They arrested me, they tortured me and beat me, and now they want to rape me. How can

I not cry and struggle?" The next night the American
came back, when I was alone. I cried again, but he forced
me to the floor and put a cloth in my mouth. He took off
my pants. I couldn't scream. I went faint, and he raped
me, and I couldn't do anything more. Later, the interpreter returned, and removed the cloth from my mouth. I
was raped again, and I didn't feel anything more. After
that, another American came—his body was smaller than
the first one's. He tortured me with electricity until I lost
consciousness. He gave me water and I regained consciousness. The second American kicked me on my
breasts and stomach. Now, I cannot feel, cannot breathe.
And he kept putting electricity in my vagina and on my
fingers. I said, "I am from a poor family, how can I tell
you anything?"

Then I was taken to Phuoc Tuong where there was
an American base, and only Americans. There, an
American lady asked me some questions. I saw other
Vietnamese girls. Then they took me back and tortured
me again. Night and day the American soldiers tortured
me. Sometimes it would be Vietnamese soldiers, but
mostly it was Americans. I was locked in a prison cell with
no window—I saw no sky, no land, nothing. Sometimes I
had a little bit of rice. After three weeks they returned me
back to the district. The first day back an American soldier came and kicked me in the mouth and my teeth
came out. I asked a Vietnamese man why they beat me, I
had committed no crime, and I asked for medicine. The
Americans came again and beat me with a stick. I was
brought back to Hoi An and kept there for a few more
weeks. Every time I was questioned, they took me to

another place, I still don't know where, not Hoi An. Every time they questioned me I was beaten. More electricity inside my body and again and again they raped me. Even now I bleed.

I spent about four years in prison altogether. There were other girls, and we used to talk about the torture. We tried to help each other. If it were not for them, I wouldn't have stayed alive. I was released at the end of 1969 and returned to my village.

Now the villagers take care of me and the government helps. I am sick, in the lungs, in the heart, and in the head. Sometimes my nose bleeds. When the weather changes, I look down, and I don't go outside. Sometimes I just lie here, and I can't breathe. Then they take me to the hospital. My fingers are very swollen and sometimes the nails fall out, from the electricity.

In 1965 I was a beautiful woman, not like now. I am forty-five and I live alone, no parents, no brothers, sisters, no husband. How can someone marry me? My father was killed by the Americans. My mother was killed by American bullets, shelled. My younger brother was killed. The boys had been playing on the road when the Americans came through, and shot them.

There is a monument in Dien Tho village that reads:
"Thuy Bo 1967. Here the American enemy barbarously
massacred one hundred and forty-five old people,
women and children. We will never forget."

MR. NGUYEN HUU

I WAS BORN IN 1910, here in Dien Tho. The massacre
was in 1967, on the 20th of December, according to the
moon calendar. South Koreans had been stationed outside
the La Tho Bridge for three days, unable to get past the
guerrillas. On the third day they made it through, and
when the people saw them, they ran. There were only
older people, women and children here. They were all
shot. They came into the houses and shot the people. The
children were torn apart by their legs. At that time, children would go around begging the Americans for sweets.
The Americans gave the children sweets and arrested the
people they thought were V.C. That day the children
asked for sweets, and they were shot. More than one hundred and forty people were killed. A few days later, after
we had buried our dead, the soldiers came back—
American, Vietnamese, South Koreans—and dug up the
bodies, and burned the village.

During the French and the Japanese occupation, I
was a guerrilla. But by the time the Americans came, I

155

just worked on the land and looked after my children.
They all died. My wife and four small children, my
brothers and their children, and many relatives were
killed. Four of my sons died at the front. Ten people in
my brother's family were killed. I am the only one left.
When I remember, I can hardly go on living.

Dien Ngoc Village

MR. HUYNG DUC AY

WHEN WE RETURNED from the evacuation center we still weren't liberated. The American and South Vietnamese forces formed a circle around us. At night, the revolutionary forces would meet. Once they had a meeting, and they were betrayed. The planes flew in, shone their lights, and killed about thirty people. In Cam Ha, when the Americans first came, all Vietnamese were labeled Viet Cong. The South Koreans shot all the Vietnamese, and tore the children apart by their legs. There is only one survivor from this massacre. One day my brother stood talking. They thought he was setting a mine, and shot him. I was just a child then.

Common grave for over one hundred people bombed in a Catholic church in Que Son on August 18, 1972. Que Son was a camp, surrounded by barbed wire and American troops. The victims had fled to the church during heavy fighting, thinking they would be safe. 1991. TAKEN BY M. HESS.

Binh Trieu Village

We visited Binh Trieu village in Quang Nam Danang province, where we had been told the American occupation was one long massacre. This is what they told us.

MR. PHAN XUAN MY

MY LET REFERS TO an American who moves very stealthily. These soldiers would spend six months away from their unit, looking for Viet Cong. They camped in the forest, on the beach—we didn't know. They moved at night. In the daytime, the Americans controlled the villages. Every morning at about eight o'clock the planes would come and drop bombs. Every day the soldiers launched mopping-up operations in our villages. They shot all the men they saw. They raped the women in secret, one at a time, because they didn't want to get caught by their officers. They even raped pregnant women. If they suspected they were V.C. they killed them, and if they resisted they killed them too. They cut off their hair—the South Koreans did everything. The young girls had to hide in the daytime.

MRS. TRAN THI TANG

I SPENT NINE YEARS in prison. There is only me and one child left. Everybody else is dead. My husband was killed during the rule of Ngo Dinh Diem. They cut off his head. I had two daughters. One was a soldier, the other a medical assistant. They were both killed during the American War. My son made his way north, and he now works in Haiphong. When I was captured, there were five Viet Cong in the shelter under my house. If you get caught, they had said, die, but say nothing. I said nothing.

MR. BAO

WHEN THE AMERICANS first came in 1964, a few military trucks were blown up by mines. And so, in retaliation the American soldiers killed every family they found in the shelters. They rounded up the women. They cut off their hair and cut off their ears, and they raped them. They threw old people in the river. About the bullets and bombs, I can't tell you. They threw fragmentation bombs on the ground. You can see how this young man's eye got twisted, because children picked up the bombs. People stayed as long as they could in the tunnels. When they came out, they were shot. Very terrible. Everything was destroyed.

I was arrested four, five times. I spent years in prison. The South Vietnamese controlled the prison. They would use powerful electricity on us. They had two lights that we had to look into. If we lowered our eyes, they beat us more. They would put a bucket over our head and beat on it, and we would be driven crazy from the noise.

After 1968 there was nobody left here.

Van Duc Nga. 1991. PHOTO BY M. HESS.

MR. VAN DUC NGA

ON MARCH 23, 1968, there was a battle here. Everybody stood by the tunnels, prepared to defy the Americans. In the mopping-up operation my mother and one aunt were killed, and I was wounded. I lost one arm, and a piece of shrapnel became lodged in my back. My genitals were destroyed—everything. I lost consciousness. The Americans shot me, and then they rescued me.

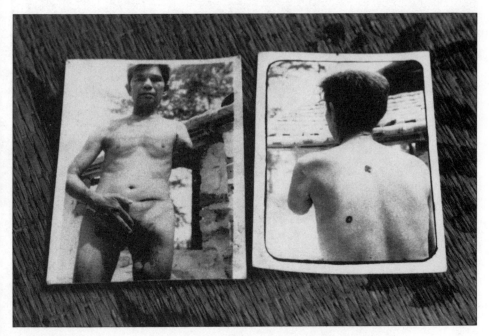

Mr. Nga showed me these photos taken of his injuries. 1991.
PHOTO BY M. HESS.

Kieu Thi Xan, and to the right is Vo Van Vuong, whose right eye is twisted after being injured by a fragmentation bomb. 1991. PHOTO BY M. HESS.

MRS. KIEU THI XAN

I WAS CAUGHT TWICE, in 1969 and 1972, for helping the revolutionary forces. I was beaten and tortured with electricity. They killed my husband, and all five of our children were killed in the war. I have no husband and no children.

MRS. TRAN THI HAI

I WAS WORKING in the fields, in 1969, when I was captured, and imprisoned for five years. First they beat me— you can see how my legs are. Then they used electricity on my breasts. Now, my legs ache and my breasts are sore. While I was in prison, the Americans came back here and shot my husband, my mother and my sister. My two surviving children had been staying with neighbors. Everything was destroyed and my family was destroyed, too. I just want to tell you this. The soldiers used to cut open people's bellies and take out the organs. I remember one woman here, she had four children and a baby at her breast, they killed her. We used to wonder who was still alive and who had been killed.

MR. VO VAN VUONG

IN 1965, I WAS A small child. The Americans were bombing, and many children were wounded and killed. When I was injured by a fragmentation bomb, an American helicopter took me to the hospital in Danang where they operated on my eye.

The Americans shot the children. The children would be playing here on this side of the river, and American soldiers from over on the other side would shoot them. The Americans would cut off the hair of the older people. They drowned people. They shot people and then threw them in the river. This lady here, they pushed her to the ground and cut off her hair. Sometimes they shot people in the eyes. And they would laugh.

Huynh Thi Pham, with a child. 1991. PHOTO BY M. HESS.

MRS. HUYNH THI PHAM

THE AMERICANS CAME in trucks. We were brought out in the sun, pushed to our knees and made to draw up our arms, as they cut off our hair. With older people, they pulled out their beards. They were laughing as they did this. We don't understand English, so we could only see what they did. At night, the Americans would come in a helicopter and shine a light on the shelters, and shoot. They dropped napalm and burned and killed many people. Women were raped. In Bin Duong village across the river, twenty-one women were raped in an afternoon by Americans, not just once but one after the other. Some died on the spot, and others died later.

My husband was taken to prison and tortured to death. He was a farmer. I had five small children then, like this one.

MRS. KIEU THI THONG

IN 1968, THE AMERICANS CAME. I lived in the second hamlet, Binh Trieu. They staged a *hanh quan*—a mopping-up operation. They took over the hamlet. They burned and destroyed three houses in my family. They killed two of my sons and a daughter. When they came to burn our house, my first son went out to stop the Americans. They killed him.

MRS. NGUYEN THI HUYNH

IN 1966 THE AMERICANS LAUNCHED an operation. They saw me as I was working in the fields, digging up sweet potatoes, so I ran, and they shot me. My husband also ran, and he was killed. The Americans were here and the Viet Cong were over there, and we were in the middle.

MR. CANH

ONE DAY IN 1965, I visited my native village, Hoa Lang. We lived in Danang at the time, about ten kilometers away. I was just a child. I remember seeing many people, soldiers from the Saigon puppet government on one side, and villagers carrying the dead bodies of children from a school. The Americans said they had bombed the school because a flag of the National Liberation Front was on the schoolgrounds, although people say this isn't true. Forty-five people were killed.

The destroyed Citadel of Hue. 1990. PHOTO BY M. HESS.

Hue

MR. HOANG LANH
a leader in the 1968 Tet Offensive in Hue.

BEFORE 1968 THE FORBIDDEN city of Hue was well preserved. The walls, the buildings, and the palace were intact. Even the gates were the original gates. There were trees planted by the Ching Dynasty in China, and sent as a present to the King of Vietnam.

The worst fighting in the Tet Offensive occurred inside the Citadel, where the American and Saigon puppet armies had their military post. It was the stronghold of the enemy. We attacked and a terrible battle ensued. The Americans sent planes in and bombed the walls and destroyed the buildings. Now the trees are gone. When you came through the main gate, you may have seen a lot of scaffolding. They put that up because of the bombs of 1968—the Tet Offensive. We call it *Mau Than*, the Year of the Monkey. The Citadel was destroyed. The monuments we lost in Hue were some of our country's most precious possessions. When we lose the prizes of our culture, we cannot put them back. Right now there is little money in Vietnam for restoration. We must look after the lives of the people.

175

We triumphed because we had the will to win. Here in Hue we conducted a mass mobilization. The people brought us food, they hid us, and took us to the road and showed us the way. Hospitals were set up to treat the wounded. Thousands and thousands of soldiers and officers were taken in by the people of Hue. We have a proverb: Our homes are destroyed—when we have defeated the enemy we can rebuild them. Everybody knows that saying.

The Americans started the war, and when they knew they were losing they kept on killing, until they were defeated. But they didn't all want war in Vietnam. There were American soldiers who resisted, who agreed with the massive anti-war demonstrations in their homeland. There were even some, for instance, who would ignore the secret shelters in the villages. They didn't want to stay in Vietnam and they didn't want to die in Vietnam, they wanted to go back to America.

But most of them were barbarous. The crimes of the United States are on our minds, even now. Our losses were inconceivable. Ten people in my family were killed by the Americans and the puppet government. They rounded up the families that had relatives in the revolutionary forces. What we remember most is the barbarity. They burned houses, they stole, they beat people, and they killed them. Thousands and thousands of people were injured, especially women. I can tell you, many women now are paralyzed, they have half a body, because they were beaten and tortured by the Americans. They tortured women with electricity. They did many, many terrible things.

We want peace so that we can rebuild our country. We lost so much in the war. What can the Americans, who are responsible for so much loss, do for my nation? We try to do away with the past and to shake hands. We try not to hate, but it's been a long hatred now.

MR. NGUYEN VAN TU

We found Tu working in a tailor shop on a quiet street in Hue. We struck up a conversation with him, and later with his mother. Tu begged us to help him get to America.

I AM EIGHTEEN YEARS OLD. My father is American. I never knew him. My mother has forgotten him. I live with my mother and foster father. When I was interviewed by the O.D.P. [*Orderly Departure Program*], I said that if my mother and foster father cannot go to America with me, that I would stay here.

But because of my face, my hair, I never think that I am Vietnamese. Everything about me looks American. And I consider myself an American. It is the country of my father, but the United States government and the O.D.P. delegation, they don't understand.

In Vietnam we always go back to our father's land, not our mother's. We say that the father's land is our land.

MRS. LE THI RI
Tu's mother

I WAS ABOUT FORTY when Tu was born. I was already married but I worked in Quang Tri. The American loved me and I loved him. So we had a child, no wedding. I lived with the soldier until my eighth month of pregnancy, and then I returned to Hue. We wrote letters, but I have lost them. When I came back to Quang Tri after Tu was born, his father was gone. The Americans had withdrawn.

I have six other children. They are okay. They are married already. Before we went to the O.D.P. interview, we sold the house, sold everything. There was nothing left. We thought we could go to America, but they didn't believe that Tu was my child. There was an American lady like you, who asked many things, asked about the papers and certificates, and about Tu's father.

I carried this child and ran away from the war. I carried him from here to Danang. If he went to America, how can I remain behind?

Because Tu was half American and half Vietnamese, the people scorned me. And some now ask why I sold my house to follow him to America. Anyway, we cannot go.

MRS. NGO THI DAO

I AM FIFTY-FIVE YEARS OLD NOW. I am from Thi
Thanh village, seven kilometers from Hue. They called it
an unsecured zone. The Americans controlled it in the
daytime and the people would hide in secret shelters, and
at night, after the Americans left, the guerrillas and
Liberation Forces were in control. This continued until
the liberation. We were only a few kilometers from the
American and South Vietnamese military post. Usually
they had a couple operations a week, and sometimes they
stayed, sometimes they withdrew. They would come by
tank or helicopter, and sometimes burned the houses. If
they came upon a shelter, they killed the people. Or they
would shout for the people to come out. If the people
were deaf or didn't understand, the soldiers would drop
mines or shoot into the shelter and kill them.

But we kept growing rice and working the fields. Of
course there were times when nobody could work the
land, when we had to run away from the fighting—what
we call *chau loan*.

Through it all, the Vietnamese people helped each
other. For example, when the people of Thi Thanh were
evacuated to the next village, their neighbors shared their
food and land, even medicine from the forest. So many in
my village were killed. We didn't have funerals. We buried
them right away. If we couldn't get them out of the house,
we buried them underneath.

I joined the Liberation Forces in 1965. Even before
that I took part in revolutionary activities. I fought in the

hills of Vinh Thuy, about five kilometers from here. As I was a deputy commander of the Special Forces of Hue and also a Party member, I went back and forth from here to the hills. They never knew who I was. The people protected me. They looked after my children, they gave me food and shelter, and helped me fight the Americans. Everything came from the people.

I lost one eye fighting, and also my left arm. When the weather changes these wounds are very painful. It was difficult to manage my children with one arm and an eye missing. My husband and my brothers, my three brothers, were sacrificed in battle. The women in my family are alone, without men.

The American and South Korean soldiers, and sometimes the South Vietnamese, raped the women, especially in the countryside. They would rape them and then cut their breasts off. Sometimes they killed the women, and sometimes they got away.

The war has been over for a long time now and I don't like to talk about it, for the American people to know, but when a young girl in one family is raped by Americans or South Koreans—how can we not be angry, even now? They should help to rebuild our country, but what can we do? So we try to forget it. It was terrible for us. You see, in one family, the unity of the family exists, parents, children, wife, husband, they have breakfast, eat meals together, and then the Americans come and kill one of them, or two of them, or three of them. How can we forget? But for life, for peace, for the future, we try to forget.

On the road from Hue City to Phu Bai,
an old American base

MRS. HO THI NY

BEFORE 1968, I LIVED about half a day by bicycle from here. The Americans came to our village, and they said it was V.C. They burned the houses and destroyed everything. I left and came here to live, from that time.

Nguyen Thi Loan, with her child. 1990. PHOTO BY M. HESS.

MRS. NGUYEN THI LOAN
Mrs. Ny's daughter, who would have been about ten years old in 1968.

BEFORE 1968, THEY WERE fighting there all the time, at Vinh Tai and Vinh Pho. In our village in 1968, there was a very big battle and many soldiers were killed. All the houses were destroyed by bombs and shells. It lasted about two weeks. I helped rescue the wounded, as a medical assistant for the Liberation Forces. I was caught by the Americans and put in jail. They took me out from a secret shelter. The South Vietnamese soldiers tortured me. They tied me up, put me in water, and connected electricity to my fingers. And they beat me many times. After a few months I was released. I was caught twice.

Such brutal suppression. I lost an aunt, who was shot by the South Vietnamese forces, and I lost many friends. My mother also went to jail, because my father had gone to the North. She was tortured and beaten too, and released after some months.

I was born on this land, and when I grew old enough, I saw the war destroy everything. That is my worst memory, and that is why I hate the enemy.

Bombed church in Quang Tri Province, just south of the 17th parallel.
PHOTO BY M. HESS.

Quang Tri Province

MR. DUY

QUANG TRI WAS LIBERATED in 1972. We suffered terrible losses because we were the last province in the South to stop the Communist troops coming from the North.

There were eighty-two days of fighting in the old city of Quang Tri. It was a beautiful city built during the Hue Dynasty, 18th century, and it was completely destroyed by bombs. It was a terrible battlefield. You can still see the old prison. Before 1972 that was where they kept people there who worked for the Communists, or who were suspected of having done so.

The inhabitants of Quang Tri all left. Some went on foot to Hue. We tried to avoid being seen by the troops. We couldn't use the road. We had to go through the rice fields, in hidden places, because, you know, Saigon soldiers, who were not very good people, they could shoot any time they wanted. Sometimes they shot young students for their clothing. They used their power for themselves. We didn't want to be near the Communist troops either, because we could get caught in crossfire and be killed. We had good reason to stay away from the soldiers. One time during the big battles of 1972, I returned to my native village, and we were surrounded by soldiers fighting for two weeks. I couldn't get out.

I had two brothers in Ho Chi Minh City, and I was a teacher under the Saigon government. The family was divided in two parts, South and North. My parents were more sympathetic to the North. During the war, in the daytime the Americans were there and the peasants worked in the fields, but at night the Communist troops came in, and they were received very warmly. Maybe the Americans couldn't see the Viet Cong. They were busy marching, looking for the enemy. I think they didn't see them.

In my village young men joined either the Communist troops or the Saigon army. Before 1954, many men followed the call of President Ho Chi Minh and went north, left their wives in the South. Then, in 1954, the country was divided in two by the 17th parallel, and we had no communication between the two sides. It was difficult for women, the war.

There were Communist soldiers who were killed at night, and the next day the villagers saw that a son or daughter was no longer there. They wanted to bury their loved one, but they were afraid. My oldest brother was a Communist soldier. We lived in the South but he had his idealism. In 1967, he was killed by Saigon troops, near our village. My mother's heart was broken. We were afraid to have a funeral, but my father found his body and carried it to the family graveyard, and now he is buried there. Because my brother was a Communist soldier, my father and older sister and my aunt were arrested several times. Not my mother, because she was blind. Many people who worked for the Communist troops at night, many people who had children who were Communist soldiers were captured and punished. My aunt was tortured and beaten so that she is crippled now.

Vietnam has three parts. In the North and South, you see rice fields stretching across the horizon, but in the central part here are mountains. This is the Truong Son range. At the U.S. base, everything came in by helicopter, even the soldiers. Their clothes were flown to Japan and the Philippines to be washed.

You lived so far away. You carried bombs, ammunition, bullets, many tanks from very far, and came here to kill anyone in the way.

MR. NGUYEN THANH KHIEM

I AM A NATIVE OF Quang Tri province. I was a soldier in the war, but from 1965 until 1972, I was in the student movement against the American occupation and the Saigon puppet government. I was arrested and spent first a year, and later several months in jail. I was so young, but they beat and tortured me for information about the student movement. I lived under different names to avoid being captured. My father and my brother were killed and our home was burned down by the Americans. My mother never recovered from the captivity and torture that she suffered, and she died very young. Under the Ngo Dinh Diem and American regimes, our family was singled out as one of the worst in the village, from the oppressor's viewpoint.

In the villages, the civilians were afraid and the Americans did whatever they wanted. The village and the land and the houses belonged to the people, but the Americans went wherever they wanted. They came into our houses and used our things. They had no respect for our ancestral table, which is sacred. They didn't know the habits or the traditions of the Vietnamese people. In our village they didn't normally burn the houses or rape the women because we were very near their base, and they wanted to maintain good relations. But the people were angry, and they helped the Liberation Forces, showed them the way.

The Americans destroyed our land. Every family has loved ones who were killed and every family suffered big losses in the war. With all the American soldiers did to the Vietnamese people, how can we not hate them? They bombed so much. Even now people get killed from unexploded bombs. Yesterday a bomb exploded at the Dong Ha stadium. People still suffer from the toxic chemicals the Americans dropped. Babies are born deformed. And they left children, the Amerasians. I feel very sorry for them, and for their mothers.

We don't like to remember the war, but sometimes we sit down like this, and we remember very clearly.

MRS. NGUYEN THI DIEN

WE SAW THE AMERICANS shoot some students who were part of the movement in our village. They put them side by side and shot them. It was near my house, and the Americans were staying in our fields. I was only ten, but I saw that. They slept in the fields and they ambushed the V.C.

WOUNDED
SOLDIERS

OVERLEAF: Seeing soldiers off to war. Taken during the U.S. War.
COURTESY VIETNAMESE PHOTOGRAPHERS ASSOCIATION (TRAN CU).

MR. LUONG QUY

Mr. Quy is the director of the department in Hanoi that cares for wounded veterans, a branch of the Vietnamese Department of Labor/Invalids and Social Affairs. I went with him to the Thuan Thanh Institute for Wounded Veterans outside of Hanoi, and also to the Hoang Long Psychiatric Institute, about one hundred and twenty-five kilometers southwest of Hanoi. He took me as well to a small textile enterprise run by and for wounded vets, subsidized by the government.

THE FIRST THING I REMEMBER as a soldier was the bombing from the B-52 planes, in Quang Nam Danang province. I started out as a teacher in the Conservancy Institute, where they train for water conservation, but in 1964 the Americans were escalating their war, and I joined the army. I went south in 1967, and stayed there for the rest of the war. I had a mission to destroy two enemy airports near Danang, Nuc Man and An Hoa.

I remember the petrol bombs and the napalm. They would burn and clear everything. Napalm burns on a big scale, and it killed many people. I was burned on my back and face. You can see the scars. The burns from the petrol bombs were treated very well, and the scars are gone. That was in 1969. I lost my thumb fighting hand to hand with

199

the Americans. You see, they are taller than I am, so when this one lunged at me with his bayonet, he got my hand.

Sometimes battles took place in the middle of a civilian population. Sometimes when we fought the Americans, after we withdrew, they came to kill the civilian people for having helped the Liberation Forces. After a battle they always rounded up the women and children and old people into concentration camps, to keep them away from the Liberation Forces. Mostly the people helped us. Everywhere we went, they gave us food and protection.

Around September 1969, when we fought the battle at Vinh Dien, after we withdrew the Americans came and rounded up the people, and they tortured them and beat them. They tied the hands and feet of the young people and set them in front of a ditch, and then shot them and kicked them into the ditch, and covered them over. About two hundred people were killed there. I tell you about this place that I know. These were Americans from the Fifth Regiment of the Marine Forces.

There were many massacres in Quang Nam Danang. There are seven villages in Go Noi. It's where two rivers meet, the island between two rivers. They used napalm to destroy all seven villages. That was also in 1969. When we first came to Go Noi, you couldn't see the sun for the trees. After three months of fighting, there was nothing left. They wanted to keep Danang, and this is what they did.

The war in Vietnam, we never forget it, we never forget it. But life goes on.

Mrs. Phuong showing me how she wears a spoon. 1990. PHOTO BY M. HESS.

Thuan Thanh Institute

DOCTOR NGUYEN NGOC CHIEU

I STARTED WORKING HERE in 1974. Most of the patients are paraplegics. Wounds of the skull and backbone are the worst. They cause many complications, like infections of the urinary tract, and stones. Patients develop ischemia and necrosis, where the flesh rots because blood isn't circulating properly in the paralyzed parts. They have respiratory problems. They have sexual problems, and many cannot have children. They cannot behave with their wives like other men. These people can't take care of themselves. They can't use the tools and implements of daily life.

The economy of Vietnam since the end of the war is very poor. We lack medical instruments, we lack medicine. We even lack supplies for their day-to-day living. We lack medical technology and a knowledge about diseases associated with paralysis.

In this province alone, Ha Bach province, 33,847 people were killed, 24,830 wounded.

MR. CHU DUC DAI

I WAS WOUNDED IN 1971, at Quang Tri. I was the head of my company. I went ahead to reconnoiter for the battle and got hit by a cannon shell from the other side. My backbone was broken and my intestine got cut in six places. I was brought back to the North, and after I recovered I stayed in the army, until 1976. Now I am the director of the Thuan Thanh Institute. I joined the army in 1959. I didn't think then that it was going to be my life, but because of the war, I stayed.

Some American veterans have come here to meet with us. According to our tradition, we welcome the enemy like a friend after the war. In battle we are enemies and we fight, but after the war we treat them as friends, because we want peace.

MRS. PHUONG

I WAS WITH THE young pioneer forces in Quang
Binh, where we had just finished rebuilding Route 21,
and the U.S. planes came to bomb the project. I was
twenty at the time, 1967. I was hit, and now I have no
arms.

I came here to live in 1970, and I got married here.
My husband was also wounded, from the French time. He
died two years ago. I have three children. Here is the first.
The others are in school.

I do everything with my legs. I use them as hands.
To write, I tie a pen to this arm, and then I can write. I
have a glove, to make a hand, but it keeps shrinking, and
they have to remake it. I use it with a spoon to cook and
eat. Housework is very difficult. I use my legs to make
rice. The babies were easy. I put them on the bed and they
took my breast. Now they help out. My daughter helps
wash my hair. When they were little, I would bring the
water here and my husband washed my hair.

Many people in my family were killed, one sister, my
aunt, three of her children—five people were killed at the
same time. It is wretched.

MR. ZUNG

I AM FORTY-THREE years old now. I was born in Nam
Ha province, about one hundred kilometers from Hanoi.
If you fought in the war with the Americans, there are
many things to remember. I went to Quang Tri when I
was twenty-one. Two years later I got hit, at Khe Sanh, in
the western part of Quang Tri. I was shot in the backbone
and I fell to the ground, and then I got hit by a cannon
shell, and it took off my leg. I had come to Khe Sanh
from Quang Binh, to fight. We had our meals in the
North and the enemy was in the South. In the night we
crossed the Ben Hai River and fought over there, and then
withdrew north again.

I woke up three weeks later in an American hospital
in Danang. They said they would treat me like an
American soldier, but they beat me. The doctors were
okay but the soldiers beat me. I was there four months,
and then I went to prison.

The prison was controlled by the South Vietnamese
puppet government. All the captured soldiers were kept in
one place, divided in two parts, the soldiers from the
North and the soldiers from the South. It was terrible. We
had no food. We had a small tin pot of rice, like this, with
a tiny bit of *mam,* fish sauce. When they felt like it, they
beat us. Every house had ninety or a hundred soldiers in
about a hundred square meters. No doctors, no medicine.
I was released in 1973, after the Paris Agreements.

I always feel pain now. I have pain all the time, and
when the weather changes, the pain gets much worse.

Every day they give me morphine to kill the pain. So much pain.

Mr. Zung just stopped talking, and even the children were silent.

MR. PHAM VAN CANH

IN 1972 I WAS SHOT in the spine, on the battlefield in Gia Lai Kon Tum, in the highlands. I had been fighting for three years. We suffered unspeakable hardship. After a battle we were always happy, though, because we had survived. I can tell you about one. We were in the Lai Forest about two kilometers from Kon Tum town, and went to the villages, Lai Khe, the concentration camps, and fought there, and then to the high points to attack the other side. The town was occupied and they were on the other side, and we attacked. The Americans brought troops to surround the three high points, and for seven days we had nothing to eat. We used to dig for roots, a meter underground. Then we attacked and liberated Pleiku, and we got rice. In six months of fighting, seven times they sent new troops to my division, we lost so many men. We took cloth to wrap them and buried them in a place we called a cemetery, but sometimes they were destroyed by bombs. There are missing Vietnamese, too.

I have been here since 1976, and tomorrow I am going to Thanh Hoa, to live with my wife and children.

Vu Trung Hieu. 1990. PHOTO BY M. HESS.

MR. VU TRUNG HIEU

I WAS INJURED in August 1968. That was the year of the hottest fighting with the Americans. I was with our Special Forces, specially trained. The enemy fought well too, so it wasn't an easy battle. I went to the front and got hit right away. I never got to fight. I got hit at the beginning of the battle.

We were in Dong Xoai, Phuoc Loc, in Song Be province. It is close to Ho Chi Minh City. I went there on foot through the western mountains, seven months. I had to go ahead to the Dong Xoai airport, to reconnoiter. I didn't see the Americans, and they shot me, right through the backbone to the other side. My comrades got me out of there and to our underground hospital. Now I am paralyzed from here down.

When I went to the South I was very young. Now I am forty-three and I still feel young. I put the past behind and think of the future. Sometimes I remember, in my dreams, terrible dreams. I never watch war films. I don't want to see them.

Mrs. Hong. 1990. PHOTO BY M. HESS.

MRS. HONG

I WAS IN THE YOUNG volunteer forces, building the roads, on the Truong Son Mountains. I was bombed in a B-52 attack on the Ho Chi Minh Trail. I had gone south in 1965 to work on the Ho Chi Minh Trail, and I got hurt in 1968, lost both arms. I met my husband there. He was a soldier passing through, and we fell in love. He went south, and I got injured. I went away and never told him, but after the war, in 1976, he went to my native land to find me, because he knew where I was from, and then he came here and we got married. He works for the center, and we live here with our two children.

MR. NGUYEN ZUAN TAI

I WAS ALWAYS IN the mountains, from 1969. I was fighting in Kon Tum and got hit, March 1971. We had the battle on Route 9, together with the battle in Kon Tum, at the high point. The fight was very long. The Americans brought troops to the high point, and we had to withdraw. We were shooting at their planes, and I got injured in the bombing, in the skull and backbone. This leg is weak, and it is difficult for me to get around. I get pain when the weather changes.

My wife is a nurse here, and I build radio parts, repair radios and electronic equipment. This is my shop. Nothing complicated. These radios come from the countryside, so they are not very modern like in the city.

Hoang Long Institute

Hoang Long means Golden Dragon, but the official name is the Rehabilitation Center of Psychiatry for War Veterans. It used to be a camp for French prisoners, and the Americans never bombed it. The director, Dr. Ha Anh, told me that more than half the patients are thought by their families to be missing in action, because they can't remember where they are from. Their families think they are dead. He said that there are no funds for rehabilitation, that the accomodations are poor, they have no space, and the equipment and technology are backward. The doctor said, "These people brought freedom to their country, but have no freedom for themselves." The patients were friendly, sang some songs about Ho Chi Minh, offered cigarettes, and three of them told me a little of their past.

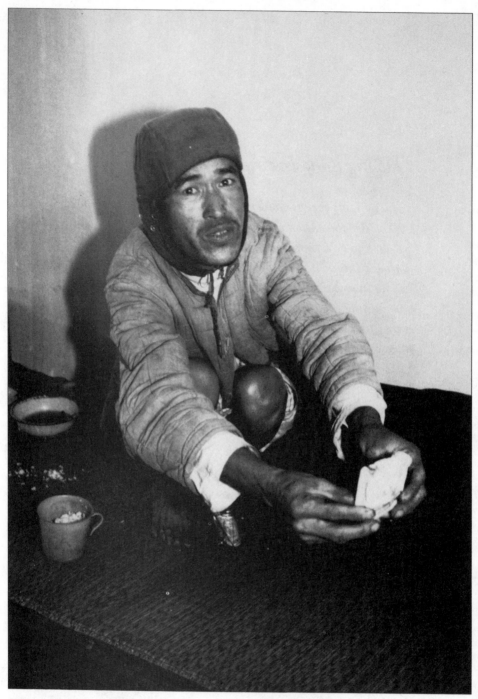

Veteran of the U.S. War at Hoang Long Institute, offering me cigarettes. 1991. TAKEN BY M. HESS.

Veteran of the U.S. War at Hoang Long Institute. 1991. PHOTO BY M. HESS.

MRS. TRUONG THI MONG

Mrs. Mong was found in Ho Chi Minh City in 1982 and brought to Hoang Long Institute. She had been a member of the Special Forces, called the Dac Cong. Tuyen says they were excellent fighters, who moved in the night. The dogs couldn't track them.

THERE IS NOBODY left in my family. I was born in Hue. I led the way for the Liberation Forces to enter the gates of the Citadel, and I led the army to fight the Americans in the airport at Tay Loc. I captured the guard outside and brought the army in. In 1968, *Mau Than,* about fifteen thousand Americans occupied Hue. My comrades and I attacked the security office, and got caught. We were in a tunnel and we fought them. Four of us were arrested, two wounded and two killed. I am the only one still alive. They killed the others. I was nineteen. They used electricity and metal sticks and they raped me, many soldiers. They gave me a disease. I was a prisoner for six years, in Quy Nhon and Phu Quoc, and then I went to Saigon. Now I can't remember very well, because I was hurt all over. I am wounded. I can't work. I can't even sew something. Before I could, but the eyes cannot see anything. I have a ring, and I say I am married by the ring. I always want to make myself beautiful, and sometimes I wear traditional Vietnamese clothing—the *ao dai.* But I am crazy.

MR. NGUYEN ZUAN TU

Mr. Sang, a director in the Hoang Long Institute, knew Mr. Tu during the war. He was one of his soldiers in the infantry, and on the march south he came down with a bad case of malaria. They thought he had died already, but he revived. Then he got wounded fighting. First they amputated his hand. Then he got gangrene and they began to remove the arm. He got gangrene again and they took the rest. With all that, and from lack of food, his malaria came back, and he was taken to the hospital. The Americans attacked the hospital and he was wounded again. There weren't enough people to take everybody out, and he was captured and brought to Bien Hoa Prison, and then Phu Quoc Island. After the Paris Agreements in 1973 he was released, treated in military hospitals, and then brought here. His family thinks he was sacrificed in battle.

I WAS BORN IN the North and came south to fight. I joined the army in 1964, in my last year of school. I got wounded in the general offensive in 1968, and the Americans attacked the hospital. Everybody fled, and whoever was left behind was taken prisoner. They beat me with sticks.

MRS. PHAM THI Y

Mrs. Y stays with her husband and three children in the family section of the Hoang Long Institute. Her husband was a soldier and is a fellow patient. The government takes care of her family.

AS A STUDENT, I WROTE SLOGANS on the walls and distributed leaflets and led demonstrations against the American government and the puppet army. In 1964, when I was fourteen, I joined the Fifth Department in Quang Nam Danang. I used to set mines to destroy tanks and the M-113 trucks. I got wounded in 1969, in an ambush. We had attacked the petrol supply in the Danang airport. They took me to the hospital, and then the puppet soldiers tortured me for information. I spent three years in prison. I remember when Ho Chi Minh read his poems over the radio, and said, "Advance, and liberation will be in our hands." Later, the army attacked the prisons and liberated us, and I came out. The Liberation Forces took me to the hospital, because they had forced soapy water down me and my belly was swollen.

I got a medal for killing the enemy. Now it's gone. I came here with two empty hands.

Underground shelter. Taken during the U.S. War.
COURTESY VIETNAMESE PHOTOGRAPHERS ASSOCIATION (TRAN CU).

NGUYEN

VAN

TUYEN

Nguyen Van Tuyen. 1991. PHOTO BY M. HESS.

Tuyen and I talked endlessly about Vietnam and the war for the weeks we worked and traveled together, and I often turned on the tape recorder. Here are some of his thoughts.

WE HAVE FOUR THOUSAND years of history, but from around 200 B.C. Vietnam was invaded by the Chinese, and they conquered us. Their domination lasted more than a thousand years, until 938 A.D. There were many, many uprisings against the Chinese, and two of them were headed by women. Trieu Thi Trinh was born in my native province, Thanh Hoa, in 248 A.D. She seized Hanoi in six months. It was called Tong Binh then. In the beginning, the story goes, she was asked to become a wife, but she said, "I don't want to be a wife. I want to ride strong winds and sail the waves, to cut off the heads of the big fish and do away with the enemies of our country. I don't want to be a slave or a concubine of men." She became a great general. The Chinese soldiers said that it is easier to fight a tiger than a lady. So, I tell you, the women in Vietnam are very strong. We always say that when the enemy comes to the house the women must fight. Everybody knows that saying. During the war, most of the villages were run by women, because the men went to the front. Women looked after the children and took their sons' and husbands' places. They joined the war, too, and now they work in the government. Mrs. Nguyen Thi Dinh is a vice president of the country. Vietnamese

225

women today come from four thousand years of foreign aggression. That's what I think.

Not counting the thousand years of Chinese domination, most of the kings in Vietnam came from my native land, Thanh Hoa. We say that when a man dies and his bones are buried in the mouth of the dragon, his son will become king. There is a dragon at Ham Rong Mountain. Ham Rong means dragon's jaw. It wants to devour the jade on the north side of the river, the Jade Mountain.

My father went to live with the local landlord's family when he was nine years old. His older brother brought him there. They had two daughters, much older than him. Every evening he had to sit at their bedside with a bamboo fan, and fan the two daughters. Every morning he had to clean out their toilet. Once they misplaced some money and they beat him, and later they found the money. He lived like a slave. One day he went to the fields to tend three buffalos. He tied them to a tree, right where his brother had left him, and went back to his family. My grandmother scolded him, gave him one good meal—what was a good meal in the past? It meant two or three bowls of potato, with manioc and some kind of wild vegetable. Then his brother took him back. My grandparents had more than ten children. They couldn't all stay at home because there was nothing to eat. My uncles, his younger brother who was killed during the war, in 1972, and the other two younger brothers, also went to live with the landlord, up to 1954. By then there was a revolution and the French were defeated, and nobody went to the landlord any more. We had land reform and started the cooperatives.

Some people say the French brought civilization to this country, but they destroyed and they stole. People tell me they brought a lot to Vietnam, like theater. But they don't know that before the revolution only the French and the rich people could come to see it. They built many nice houses in Hanoi, but it was they who lived in them. They say they brought money from France to build those houses. No. They took our wealth and they used our cheap labor. They thought they could stay here forever. Ninety-eight percent of the population couldn't go to school. They were illiterate. Even the landlord had to be very rich to send his children to school. The French took rubber, wood, everything out of Vietnam. They ordered us not to grow rice, so they could plant trees to bring back to France. In 1945, two million people died in North Vietnam alone. You can't say they brought civilization to the Vietnamese people, no. Many South Vietnamese people say that, who worked for the French. They got rich. They can say they got civilization from the French. How many people like that are there in Vietnam? Very few. Later, people in South Vietnam lived on American aid, people who worked for the puppet government. Others were prostitutes, also aided by the Americans. And the upper class in Saigon lived well. Everyone else, sometimes they had a little bread, a good meal today, and tomorrow they have nothing.

When my father married my mother in 1948, they had nothing. One day my mother went to work for the landlord for a few days, working the rice. When she returned, he was gone. He had joined the army. He got wounded, he came back, and I was born at that time, end of 1952. From 1954 in North Vietnam, until 1964, we had a short period of peace. You can say peace because there was no enemy and we were building the country. But we still sent people and rice to the South, and to Laos and Cambodia. They were fighting Diem and the U.S. advisers. In 1964, the Americans began to bomb North Vietnam.

I was born three kilometers from the Ham Rong Bridge. It connects the North and the South, and it was bombed constantly. There were six bridges. If one was destroyed or three were destroyed, they had the others. It used to be very prosperous by the bridge, with buildings, stores, a station. Everything is gone. When the bombs came I climbed up trees to watch. I was very young, twelve, thirteen years old. The first time was in March 1965. For two days they bombed the Ham Rong Bridge, and forty-seven planes were shot down. Many planes were shot down here during the war. They could never completely destroy the bridge.

I remember the first person I saw killed, a woman who lived two or three hundred meters from us. She had gone to the market, which was on the other side of the river. On the way back she got hit. Part of her skull was cut out, and you could see her brain was still pulsing. The people cried and her mother cried, but I stood watching, fascinated. I saw many people die after that, different times, different ways, in a month, in a year. It went on four years, the first bombing. By 1972 I was already grown, and saw it differently.

The first time I saw an American, he was already dead. My friend and I swam the river to see. Another time, I ran with the people to capture a pilot, and when we arrived, right away the planes came back to drop bombs. They wanted to send in a helicopter to rescue him, but they couldn't. The people put him on a buffalo cart and brought him to Thanh Hoa City. When he came through our village, there was a man whose son had died at the front, and he took up his scythe, like this, to kill him, but the people held him back. Mostly the pilots were killed when the plane exploded.

I remember a train that was destroyed in the station. It was bringing rice from the North, and rice was everywhere. We carried it to the school—the school was alreay evacuated—and the rice on the road, nobody took it. The people were hungry, but they knew that rice was for the soldiers at the front.

All the villages had a guard tower, and a gong made from a bomb. When the American planes came, the guards would beat the gong, and we went to the shelter. People destroyed their houses and used the wood to build shelters underground. We were bombed day and night. The planes came, the villagers went to the shelter. The bombing ended, the planes left, they went back to work. They just did it.

We went to school. We had a hut under the trees, by the river, and around it we built up the earth, about two meters, so the bombshells wouldn't hit us. There was a hat we had, made of straw. When the planes flew overhead, we put it on, to protect against the bomb pieces and shells that came down from the sky. We each had a little container with peepee water, so in case they dropped toxic chemicals you smelled this and it made you vomit. We had a little bag with books and paper, and we went to school. We studied, the planes came and we went to the shelter, finish bombing we studied again, and we went home. Most of the grown-ups had a rifle. The teacher would stand at the entrance to the shelter to shoot the planes. As I got bigger, I helped carry shells, and we built *cong su,* strongholds for the guns.

I knew who the Americans were. I knew who was Eisenhower, starting from secondary school. And later on Kennedy, and when he was killed Johnson took his place. I knew who was Nixon, and then Gerald Ford, and then Carter.

I have an aunt who lost two sons, and then they told her the third one died. She didn't believe it. Every day she laid the ancestral table and put down food for his return. My father would tell her, "No, he is dead, he died on the front." And she said, "My young brother, you don't know anything. He will come back." He didn't. Now she worships the Buddha. It was too big for her, too much suffering. Not enough tears for crying. For the third one she could not cry. Many stories. I lost many people in my family. Three cousins from this aunt, one from another sister of my father. My mother's sister's son, who was my closest friend, died in 1979, in the war with China. The elder brother of my father, whose son was killed in the Battle of Saigon one day before liberation, which was April 30, 1975. And I had one childhood friend who died at Quang Tri, another at Quang Ngai. My father's younger brother joined the army in 1959. His wife had their first child in 1960. The second time he came to visit they had a second child, I think in 1965, and the third time he came only one night, and he had to go south the next day. Their third child was born in 1969. In 1972 he was killed at Quang Tri. My aunt says, "I was married to your uncle for fourteen years, but in fact we didn't live four hundred days together." Many people in my village waited—how many years? They waited fourteen, twenty years for their husbands and children.

I wasn't yet eighteen when I left my family to join the war. I had three, four months of training, and then they brought us by truck to the South. On the road we sang songs, we would talk, chat. We were cheerful. First we went to Quang Binh, in the forest, for three months. We stayed in the villagers' houses. Then we walked, for months. Along the Ho Chi Minh Trail I walked to Khe Sanh, almost to the front lines, the soldiers surrounding the Americans at Khe Sanh. I was part of the infantry forces. Every day we waited outside their camp, and when the Americans appeared from inside, we would shoot. In Vietnamese we say *ban tia*—it means to shoot anybody, everyone you saw. That is where I joined the battle. It was fierce, very hard. It was very hot, too. Everybody had a shift. We would dig a hole quickly, and stand up in it with our gun. We always went three by three. We stood there eight, nine hours, sometimes more. Then the next shift came, and we would go to sleep.

I fought in Khe Sanh about three months, and then they sent us to Do Mieu and Con Tien, and we fought the Saigon puppet army. I think that was the worst time in my life. We stayed in the tunnel. First they came to

Marching south. Taken during the U.S. War.
COURTESY VIETNAMESE PHOTOGRAPHERS ASSOCIATION (TRAN CU).

drop bombs, to clear the battlefield, and then the soldiers came down from helicopters. But they always bombed first, not just one day, two days, they bombed three, four days. All the land explodes and the energy tears people up. Blood comes through the nose, through the mouth, through the ears. In my village I have friends, my age or older, they returned from the front and they look stupid, because they are concussed, bomb-shocked. When people talk they don't hear, so they look stupid. Once at the front, more than half my friends and comrades were killed by bombs, in three days. We kept them there in the tunnel. We would wrap them in something, whatever we had, and then stand for a moment, looking for those who had passed from life. Then we continued to fight. After the fight we buried them and tried to find a piece of wood, to scratch their name. We made a map of where we buried people, so that later on we could put them in a cemetery. At the front, if your comrade was killed you must bring his body out. You cannot leave the bodies of your dead friends at the front. Sometimes we were fighting over a few meters, back and forth I don't know how many times. In the morning it was ours, by noon they had it, in the afternoon we took it again. Very fierce battle. For weeks we would take and withdraw.

Many interesting and fantastic stories. I told you about the time our platoon went to bathe in the stream and they started bombing, and some of us lost our clothing, so we had to share. We would look at one another and laugh. For Tet, the villagers gave us festival cakes and sweets. Sometimes we found a blossoming apricot branch to set out. We sang songs and listened to

the radio—which we took from the enemy—and waited
for Ho Chi Minh to welcome the New Year. Often we
had no food. Sometimes we had enough. When we went
to the villages after fighting, the people gave us a good
meal. Four, five big bowls of rice we could eat, with fish
sauce. The people helped us. If not, we couldn't have
stayed. One time I lost my platoon and I wandered
through the forest for two weeks. I had nothing to eat.
Then I found another unit. In that case, if the first battalion doesn't know that you are all right, they might
notify your family that you were sacrificed at the front.

In our soldiers' life, you know, we shared everything.
If you got a letter from your love, you could read it to
your friends. If you had food from the people, you gave
everyone. Because, you see, you don't know when you
could be killed. You don't know if tomorrow you will still
be alive, or even the next moment. When your friends
die, so many, you feel shocked. Yesterday he talked with
you, told funny stories, shared with you one ear of corn,
and today he is killed. Such sorrow, terrible sorrow, bad
days of war.

Sometimes I see old friends and we talk about the
past. And sometimes we drink beer, or a little bit of
brandy or whiskey, and we say, we didn't have this back
then—but sometimes we had. We would attack the
enemy camp, and after we seized it we took everything.
There were all these boxes with food, but we didn't know
what they were because we didn't read English. We would
taste it and say, "Okay, I will try it first, and if it's poison
only I will die. If not, I will have more to eat than you."
Very funny.

If you compare the conditions of the American soldiers with ours, theirs were better. They had water for showers brought in by helicopter—when we saw that, we knew they would never win the war. We came there on foot, with a gun and some bullets and a shovel, two sets of clothing, our rice, dry food, and a canteen of water. We had nothing else. At that time they were the enemy. They came here to invade my country and I had to fight them. That is all I thought. I didn't know that these Americans were tricked by their government into coming here.

The American government asks for missing bones in Vietnam, and they say we have to help find them. Why don't they talk to the women who told you how they lost their husbands, how they lost their brothers, how they lost their children at the front and never saw their bones? Why should we help them? They have the right to come to Vietnam and start a war, but we have no right to defend our country? They can tell the world they are right, but it's not true. So why should we help the Americans find their bones? But we do that for humanity.

In Vietnam, when people are born and raised on the land, they always belong to this land. They don't want to live someplace else, even if it is a better life. That is Vietnamese. When I came back from the front to my village, I felt very close.

In 1972, I went to Hanoi to study. During the bombing we were evacuated, but they were bombing the countryside, too. Many people were killed in the village I went to. I had two friends, they were staying in a house—we stayed in people's houses. In front of the house was a shelter. A bomb dropped right on the shelter and made a huge crater. A mother and her five children were killed. We found our two friends in the fields, too scared to come back. The six people, we didn't even find one piece. The husband, these children's father, was fighting at the front. B-52 planes bombed during the night, and no one could escape. Even while they slept, in their dreams, they were bombed. If you were still alive, you ran to the shelter. If you were killed, you were already dead.

The smart bomb has two purposes, to destroy and to kill. The fragmentation bombs kill people. Phosphorus and napalm bombs burn the land and the houses, and they burn people. They burn the trees—phosphorus sticks on the skin. It's like a mystery, the way it burns.

I didn't think the war would end in 1975. I had fought the Americans and I knew them. Their strength was that they had bombs and planes. We used to say the bombs have eyes. So why were they defeated? Because the war in Vietnam was a war of the people. All the people joined the war. We knew we would win but we didn't know when. Our grandfathers and our fathers had just defeated the French, and they had nothing, not even guns. The Vietnamese fight well.

The Americans and South Vietnamese in 1975 said that when we conquered the South it would be a blood-bath, after the Vietnamese forces came into the city. But that can't happen, because if you kill the people, with whom do you live? It's wrong. Never can happen, I don't think. Except Pol Pot. But for the Vietnamese, never. The American soldiers were foreign troops. The soldiers of Thieu—we called them that—were on the other side but they were brothers. During the wars with China, during the war with the French, during the war with America, there were always some who followed the invader. We forgive them. They can't go to America to live, they can't go to China—some go, but I tell you, no matter how much money they make, no matter how many houses they own, they never feel that is their land. Here we have hardship, difficult life, but this is our land. That's the real Vietnamese. The other kind, they can go, but if they stay here, we forgive them. More than a million and a half South Vietnamese soldiers stayed, more than two thirds of the forces of the South Vietnamese government. They can't all leave. In fact, some of them have high positions in the government. Nguyen Xuan Oanh, who was a deputy prime minister in the Saigon puppet government, is an adviser to Nguyen Van Linh, the General Secretary of the Communist Party. I just tell you what I think, not what others are thinking.

After 1975, I cannot say we have become poorer. It is better. But the needs of the people during the war are quite different from our needs now. Life has come up. For instance, during the war I didn't need the best clothing, like this. I only needed one ordinary set of clothing, to go to the front, to work the land. Now I need something nice, for the festival, to visit. So it's a different life.

The Americans occupied this country, destroyed it, committed horrors here. Twenty years ago you came here with helicopters, with guns, with planes, with rockets and bombs, and then you were the enemy. But we want to shake hands today. Vietnamese people have a tradition. After war we want a good life, happiness, we want peace. War destroys everything. Peace, no matter how poor you are, you can build something. Slowly, but you can build. So we try to forgive America for what they did, to build our country and to build world peace. We defeated the Chinese three, four, five times, and each time we laid down a carpet of flowers, for them to come back in peace. American, Chinese, or anybody else that comes in friendship, it's okay.